Introduction

Reading Section

Writing Section

Reading Section

Writing Section

The Essentials of GCSE AQA English covers AQA GCSE English Specification A. As a revision guide, it focuses on the skills and material which are externally assessed and covers all the information students need to pass the exam.

Students following this course will sit two exam papers (on different days) and each paper has two sections. This book is divided up in exactly the same way to allow students to prepare for each paper / section separately.

Each section in the guide begins by clarifying the nature of that particular part of the exam: the skills that are being assessed, the time allowed to answer each question, the number of questions that must be answered, and what the examiners will be looking for in the students' answers.

The guide looks at the different types of questions that may arise in the exam and explores the skills and language needed to respond appropriately. This ensures that the students know exactly what they are being asked to do.

Tasks and activities are included to help students prepare for the exams and practise their reading and writing skills, along with hints and tips to help them succeed.

Additional helpful information is given, including useful language terms, and common spelling, grammar and punctuation errors. This information appears at the beginning of the book to provide a useful revision reference when studying for either paper.

The Essentials of GCSE AQA English is written by an expert team of English teachers / examiners, with over 60 years' teaching experience between them: Paul Burns, Mary Crook, Jan Edge and Philippa Ronan.

Their experience as GCSE examiners means that they have an excellent understanding of the criteria used for marking English papers and are able to offer invaluable advice on how to perform well in the exam.

Contents

Common Errors

Punctuation and Grammar

Punctuation and grammar are very important in order to convey meaning through a piece of writing. You will be expected to use punctuation and grammar correctly in the exam. The following information is provided to help you when you are writing your answers in the English exam (and in your other exams). Read the information through and make sure you understand it.

Full Stops (.)
Full stops separate sentences. Without them writing does not make sense.

Commas (,)
Commas are used to mark smaller breaks or pauses than full stops. They must not be used to link two separate statements which could stand alone as sentences, unless a connective (e.g. 'and' or 'because' (see page 34)) or a word like 'who', 'which' or 'that' is used, for example…

> I fed the dog, which was hungry. ✓
> I fed the dog, because it was hungry. ✓
> I fed the dog, it was hungry. ✗

Commas are used to mark off parts of a sentence which give extra information, but are not necessary for the sentence to make sense, for example…
Amy , having eaten ten bananas, was feeling sick.
Tom , the football captain, scored two goals.
The phrases in red could be taken out and the sentences would still make sense.

Commas are used to list items, for example…
> He bought sugar, butter, eggs and flour.

Commas are also used to introduce speech, for example…
> 'I've had enough,' he cried, 'I'm going.'

Question Marks (?)
Question marks come at the end of questions. They are used in direct speech, but not in indirect (reported) speech, for example…

> 'Did you see Lizzie at the party?' asked Darren. ✓
> Darren asked me if I'd seen Lizzie at the party? ✗

Colons (:)
Colons are used before an explanation or example, for example…
> The marathon was a very long race: 26 miles!

Colons also appear before a list, for example…
> I got lots of presents: a book, a hat, loads of CDs.

The part before the colon must be a complete sentence, but the part after it does not need to be.

Semi-colons (;)
Semi-colons are used to show that two sentences are closely related, for example…
> The game may be cancelled; it depends on the weather.

The parts before and after the semi-colon must be complete sentences.

Apostrophes (')
Apostrophes are used to show omission or contraction (usually in speech or in informal writing). The apostrophe replaces the missing letter(s), for example…

> He shouldn't have eaten that. (Should not = shouldn't)
> You'll never understand. (You will = you'll)
> Mark's finished his work but Rachel's still doing hers. (Mark has = Mark's, Rachel is = Rachel's)

Apostrophes are also used to show possession (ownership). If the owner is singular, (or plural (more than one) but does not end in 's' - e.g. sheep, men, children), add an apostrophe and an 's' to the word that indicates the owner, for example…

> The cat's tail (i.e. the tail of the cat)
> The boy's shoes (i.e. the shoes of the boy)
> The children's books (i.e. the books of the children)

If there is more than one owner and the word indicating the owners ends in 's', simply add an apostrophe at the end, for example…

> The cats' tails (i.e. the tails of the cats)
> The boys' shoes (i.e. the shoes of the boys)

Confusing Words

Done / did, and seen / saw
These words are often used incorrectly.

> I did it   I saw it   ✓
> I have done it   I have seen it   ✓
> I done it   I seen it   ✗

Could, would, should, ought to, might
These are modal verbs. They are never followed by 'of'. They are followed by 'have', for example…

> I could have won the race.   ✓
> I could of won the race.   ✗

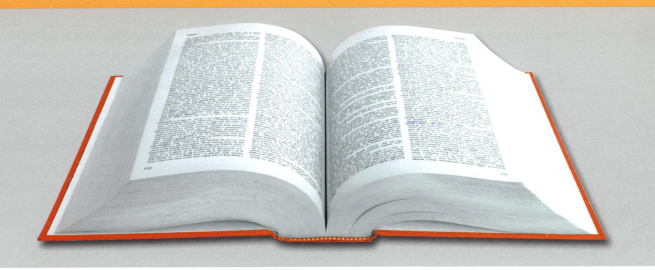

Spelling

It is important that you spell and use words correctly in the exam. The following list contains words which are frequently misused. It will help you if you read through these words and learn the correct ways to spell them and use them.

Accept – to receive: 'I accept your gift with thanks'.
Except – without: 'all the boys except John went'.

Aloud – out loud: 'read your work aloud'.
Allowed – permitted: 'chewing is not allowed'.

Hear – to hear with your ears: 'I can hear music'.
Here – in this place: 'It's over here'.

Its – belonging to it: 'the cat licked its paws'.
It's – short for 'it is': 'it's a long way home'.

Lay / lie – The past tense of 'lie' is' lay', 'last night I lay on my bed for a while'.
In the present tense you 'lay a table' or, if you are a hen, 'lay an egg'.

No – opposite of 'yes': 'no, I didn't like it'.
New – opposite of old: 'it's a new bag'.
Know / knew – being aware of something: 'I didn't know Michael knew about it'.

Passed – a verb: 'I passed all my GCSEs'.
Past – a noun indicating a previous time: 'it's all in the past now'.
(Also used in phrases such as 'he went past' or 'they are past their best'.)

Practice – a noun: 'netball practice is cancelled'.
Practise – a verb: 'if you practise hard you might get into the team'.
(The same rule applies to advice / advise.)

Quite – fairly, a bit: 'the essay was quite good'.
Quiet – silent: 'I knew there was something wrong because the class was so quiet'.

Right – opposite of wrong: 'that is the right way'.
Write – what you do in an exam. Someone who writes is a writer: 'she writes well'.

There – in that place: 'I'll be there soon'. (Also used in phrases such as 'there is', 'there are' etc.)
They're – 'they are' (the apostrophe shows that the 'a' is missing): 'they're not friends'.
Their – belonging to them: 'they left their bags on the bus'.

Too – excessively: 'we had too many sweets'.
Two – the number: 'the two bears were sad'.
To – towards: 'he went to bed'. (Also part of the infinitive of a verb, 'to do', 'to think' etc.)

Where – a place: 'where did you say it was?'.
We're – 'we are' (the apostrophe shows that the 'a' is missing): 'we're not sure'.
Wear – used with clothes etc.: 'I will wear my gold earrings'.

Whether – if: 'I don't know whether to go or not'.
Weather – the sun, wind, rain etc.: 'the weather was terrible'.

Whose – belonging to whom: 'whose coat is it?'.
Who's – 'who is' or 'who has': 'who's that boy? Who's dropped that coat?'

Language Terms

The following language terms are used in all kinds of writing. You will have used these terms in class (especially when discussing poetry) to describe the techniques that writers use in their work. The following list is a reminder of the main techniques and why a writer might use them. The terms are mentioned throughout the revision guide, so it will help you to read through them before you start revising.

Accent: the way a character would sound if they were speaking aloud, e.g. a cockney accent is used by most of the characters in *EastEnders*. Accent can be conveyed through the use of non-standard spelling, e.g. 'ah wunder'd where tha'd bin', to portray a Yorkshire accent. *Used to show where a character is from and to indicate something about his / her way of life.*

Adjectives: describe nouns, e.g. great, harsh, excrutiating, yellow, bright. *Used to add more detail to the noun, and to build images in the reader's mind.*

Adverbs: describe verbs (the action) and often end with 'ly', e.g. carefully, quietly, quickly. *Used to add more detail to an action.*

Alliteration: repetition of a sound at the beginning of words, e.g. 'big balls bounced'. *Used to stress certain words or phrases.*

Assonance: rhyme of the internal vowel sound, e.g. 'pull and push', 'cat in the bag'. *Used to slow the reader down and emphasise certain words.*

Contrast: a strong difference between two things. *Used often to highlight opposition.*

Dialect: the words and grammar that speakers use. Regional dialects differ from the Standard English dialect. Each dialect has its own special words and ways of using grammar. *Used to show which social group a character belongs to. A writer might give two characters different dialects to show that they are from different social groups, and to create a sharper contrast.*

Exclamations: show anger, shock, horror, surprise and joy, e.g. 'I won!'. *Used to portray emotions.*

Imagery: the words are so descriptive they allow you to create a picture in your mind. *Used to involve the reader in the moment being described.*

Irony and sarcasm: the use of words to imply the opposite of their meaning. *Used to make fun of people or issues. e.g. if your friend had chicken pox and you said to him / her, 'Your skin looks nice today', you would be using irony / sarcasm.*

Juxtaposition: the positioning of two words, phrases or ideas next to or near each other. *Used to highlight a contrast between two words, phrases or ideas.*

Metaphor: an image created by referring to something as something else, e.g. 'the army of ants was on the rampage'. Here the ants are referred to as an army. *Used to give additional information to the reader to create a particular effect or to emphasise a point.*

Onomatopoeia: a word that sounds like what it describes, e.g. splash, boom, click. *Used to appeal to the senses of the reader, in this case their hearing.*

Personification: making an object / animal sound like a person, giving it human qualities, e.g. 'the fingers of the tree grabbed at my hair as I passed'. *Used to enable the reader to identify with what is being personified and helps to create a specific image.*

Puns (also referred to as **play on words**): words used in an amusing way to suggest other meanings, e.g. 'She's parking mad!' *Used to entertain and amuse, and to imply another meaning. Puns are often found in newspaper headlines and shop names.*

Questions (interrogatives): show that the writer wants the reader to consider the question, or that they themselves are considering the question. *Used to show a range of things about a character such as inquisitiveness, upset and confusion.*

Received Pronunciation: the accent used by many national newsreaders. You cannot tell which part of the country a Received Pronunciation speaker comes from. This accent is seen as prestigious (impressive) and is associated with social groups that are well-educated and wealthy.

Repetition: when words, phrases, sentences or structures are repeated. *Used to stress certain words or key points in the piece of writing.*

Rhetorical questions: questions that don't need an answer, e.g. when your teachers ask 'do you think that is funny?' they do not expect you to answer. Such questions do not require an answer; the answer is obvious. *Used to make the reader think about the question that has been asked.*

Rhyme: the use of rhyming words which affects the sound patterns. Sound patterns can be regular or irregular. *Used to adjust the tone of a poem, or to emphasise a point such as in newspaper headlines.*

Rhythm: the beat of the writing (mainly poems) when read aloud: fast or slow, regular or irregular. *The rhythm of the writing (poem) can add to its overall effect.*

Simile: a comparison of one thing to another that includes the words 'as' or 'like', e.g. 'the man was as cold as ice', 'the pain was like a searing heat passing through her'. *Used to give additional information to the reader to create a particular effect or to emphasise a point.*

Standard English: the conventional or 'correct' use of words and grammar in the English language.

Superlatives: words which express the best or worst of something. They often end in 'est' or have 'most' or 'least' before them, e.g. 'lowest', 'happiest', 'most beautiful', 'least stylish'. *Used to emphasise a point.*

Symbols and symbolism: a symbol is an object which represents an abstract idea, e.g. a dove symbolises peace, red symbolises danger. *Used to create a stronger, more vivid image, or communicate an idea indirectly.*

Tone: the overall attitude of the writing, e.g. formal, informal, playful, angry, suspicious, ironic. *Used to allow the emotions of the author, or the character in the writing, to be expressed.*

Exam Overview

The Paper

The GCSE AQA English exam consists of two papers which the students sit on separate days. Each paper is divided into two sections: reading skills and writing skills.

Paper	Section	Section Title	Questions	Time Allowed
1	A	Reading Non-fiction and Media Texts	Answer all questions	1 hour
1	B	Writing to Argue, Persuade or Advise	Answer one question	45 minutes
2	A	Reading Poetry from Different Cultures	Answer one question	45 minutes
2	B	Writing to Inform, Explain or Describe	Answer one question	45 minutes

The Questions

Read the exam paper and each question very carefully. Look out for small words in the questions such as 'and' and 'or'. Make sure you understand exactly what the question is asking you to do before you begin to answer it.

You must make it very clear which question you are answering in the exam. Give the number of the question you have chosen to answer. In Paper 1 Section A, where you must answer all the questions, make it obvious where one answer finishes and the next one begins. Do not let one answer run into another.

The Importance of Planning and Checking

In each section of the exam, you should spend about five minutes at the beginning planning your answer, and five minutes at the end checking your answer.

It is very important and very beneficial to plan your answer. Examiners like to see that you have planned your work. A plan reminds you to structure your work in paragraphs, and helps to produce a good answer which is clear, logical and flows well.

It is equally as important to check your work. Read it through and ensure you have covered everything you wanted to. Make sure that the words you have chosen put across the idea or effect that you intended

them to. Check your spelling and punctuation – it is easy to make mistakes when you are under pressure.

Tips to Help you Prepare for your English Exam

- Identify errors that you frequently make and practise until you are no longer making them. Use the information on pages 4 and 5 to help you.
- Learn the terms for the language techniques listed on pages 6 and 7 – what they describe, why they are used, and how the terms are spelt.
- Work through the Exam Preparation and Exam Practice tasks in this guide.
- Try writing answers to the example questions that are given throughout the book, within the time allowed in the actual exam.
- Read over some of the work you have done in school (especially work done under exam conditions) and think about how it could be improved.

Remember that the information in this revision guide is not intended to replace what you have learnt in class, just to provide you with key points to help with your revision.

Try to stay calm in the exam and enjoy writing your answers. Make the most of the chance to express yourself.

Paper 1

Section A:

Section B:

Reading Non-fiction and Media Texts

The Exam Questions

In Section A of Paper 1 you will be tested on your reading response to non-fiction / media texts. You will be provided with two theme-related non-fiction / media texts on a loose insert inside the exam paper (you will not see the texts before your exam). You will be asked two questions (perhaps with several parts to them) on these texts. Each question will tell you how many marks it is worth in brackets (e.g. *(8 marks)*); this will give you an idea of how much you are expected to write. The questions might also give you a bulleted list of points to consider. Make sure you cover all the points listed, as these are what the examiner will be looking for in your answer.

You must answer **all** the questions, and all the parts to the questions. It is recommended that you spend about one hour on this section of the paper.

What is the examiner looking for?

The examiner wants to see that you can read and understand non-fiction and media texts. It is important that you present your answers clearly and logically; the examiner must be able to read your handwriting and understand what you are saying. Your responses to reading media and non-fiction texts must show that you can do the following:

- Read with insight and understand what the text is about.
- Understand the writer's ideas and attitudes.
- Discuss and develop your interpretations of the texts.
- Make appropriate references to the texts.
- Explain the obvious 'surface' meaning and also try to read 'between the lines' for a meaning on a deeper level.
- Make a personal response to the text.
- Distinguish between fact and opinion.
- Follow an argument by identifying implications and recognising inconsistencies.
- Compare texts.
- Pick out details from the texts effectively, using references and quotations to back up the points you make.
- Understand and evaluate how linguistic, structural and presentational devices (e.g. text in italics or bold, use of pictures) are used for effect.
- Recognise and understand linguistic features such as irony and sarcasm.
- Comment on how the language varies and changes.
- Consider the effects of the writer's use of language and the way he / she creates mood, atmosphere etc.

Helpful Hint

Make sure you answer the question properly. Answer the question that is asked, not the one you would like it to be.

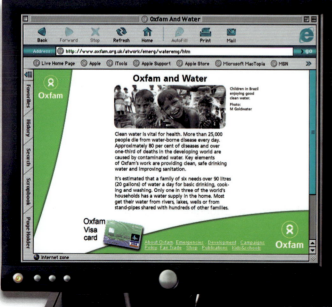

Many thanks to Oxfam for use of material: © Oxfam GB Reproduced by permission.

Non-fiction and Media Questions

Many Thanks to DEFRA for permission to use this leaflet.

In the exam, the texts you are given may contain pictures, photographs or other graphics. You may be asked to comment on any feature of the text (e.g. presentation or layout), not just the words used so if you think the images or layout add something to the information in the text, say so.

There is usually one question which asks you to compare the texts; this means that you must write about the texts equally, drawing attention to similarities and differences between them.
Try to work out which text you think is most effective and say why.

Key Words in a Question

It is helpful to look out for key words in the exam questions. The following key words tell you straightaway what the question is asking you to do:

What   - describe something
Why   - explain something
How   - identify the writer's techniques
Discuss   - suggest different meanings
             or viewpoints
Comment - analyse something and read
             'between the lines'.

It may help you to highlight or underline the key words in each question so that you can see at a glance what the main point of each one is.

Helpful Hint

Read the questions before you read the texts. The questions will tell you exactly what to look out for and will enable you to focus your reading on the information you need for your answers.

Exam Preparation

Highlight or underline the key words in these questions.

1. Comment on how the writer uses facts and opinions to support the points he is making.
2. What is the writer's attitude towards fox-hunting, and how do you know this?
3. Discuss the ways in which language is used in the article.

What are Non-fiction and Media Texts?

Non-fiction Texts

A non-fiction text refers to any text that is factual (not made up). This covers many types of texts. It is impossible to give a complete list of the different types of non-fiction texts because there are so many, but they include all media texts and texts like the following:

- cooking recipes
- history essays
- hard-hitting articles stating opinions
- travel books
- diaries or journals of a real person

- lists of instructions
- dictionary definitions or encyclopaedia entries
- reports about particular events or incidents
- biographies and autobiographies. (A biography is a written account of a person's life, written by someone else. An autobiography is a written account of a person's life, written from the viewpoint of that person and usually written by that person.)

You may get any of the texts listed here in your exam, however there are many more texts which come under 'non-fiction'. Non-fiction texts can include anything which is not a poem, story, novel or play. They are all around us in the form of leaflets, information sheets, books, junk mail and many more items.

Non-fiction texts are written to inform, explain, persuade, advise, argue or describe.

Exam Preparation

Try regularly reading some of the non-fiction texts which you see around you. You should also try to work out which techniques the writers use to get their information across in an interesting and appealing way.

Media Texts

The term 'media text' refers to a text that expresses fact, or expresses opinion in a factual way (see page 23). It covers many types of texts and includes the following:

- newspaper articles, reports, features, editorials or letters
- magazine articles, reports, features or letters
- images and cartoons (with captions)
- pamphlets and leaflets
- travel brochures
- adverts
- promotional material / literature
- web pages

You may get any of the texts listed above in this section of the exam.

Media texts may inform you about something, describe something to you, argue a case, advise you on something, explain something to you, or simply entertain you.

A large proportion of media texts however try to persuade you to do something such as donate money to a charity, buy a product, or agree with a particular point of view. For example, newspapers often want you to agree with their opinions, and adverts want you to be persuaded to buy a product.

You need to think about the techniques used in media texts to assist in persuading you to do something or getting you to agree with something.

Exam Preparation

In order to become familiar with media texts, try to read a variety of them every week. Travel brochures are free from travel agents, and you should also be able to get hold of leaflets free of charge when you are out and about.

Writing Your Answer

Remember that you have only limited time (one hour) in which to plan and write your answer to this section of the exam. Therefore you cannot waste any time.

It is important to learn how to extract information from texts quickly and efficiently. Follow these steps:

- Read the questions so you know what to look out for.
- Read through both texts once and try to work out the main points of each.
- Re-read the texts to look for the information requested in the questions. This is called scanning.
- Underline the key points / pieces of information you need to answer the questions.
- Think about the language, layout and tone of the texts.
- Spend about one quarter of your time reading the texts and planning your answers.

The PEE Technique

Always use the 'PEE' technique in your answers. You may have referred to this as 123 or another term which indicates that you must have a three part response to your answers:

P Point (make a point)
E Evidence (use a quote or example from the text to provide evidence of your point)
E Explanation (explain how the evidence illustrates your point).

When writing your answer, do...
- begin confidently. Your first sentence should show the examiner that you know exactly what the question is asking you to do.
- make sure that every sentence you write is relevant to the question and make sure you are concise; avoid 'waffling' or repeating yourself.
- use the correct technical terms when necessary (see pages 6, 7 and 15).
- try to use impersonal language like 'It seems' or 'It appears' rather than 'I think'. This will make you sound sure of yourself.
- be analytical. Suggest why certain words / pictures have been used and comment on their effect.
- use examples from the text and layout to back up your points, and use brief quotes which clearly illustrate the points you are making.
- write in accurate English. Be particularly careful not to mis-spell words which are in the text or on the question paper – there is no excuse for this!

When writing your answer, do not...
- write out the question. This is a complete waste of your precious time.
- re-tell the content of the text – this wastes time.
- copy large chunks from the text. Instead, show that you understand the text by explaining the most important points in your own words.

Helpful Hint

Spend some time reading the texts, underlining key points and making brief notes.

Non-fiction and Media Terms

There are a number of technical terms which you should be familiar with when you analyse non-fiction and media texts. It is important that you know these terms so that you will be able to make your points more clearly, and the examiner will be able to understand what you are trying to explain.

Broadsheet — A large-sized newspaper (e.g. *The Telegraph*), which reports news in detail and has a formal tone.

Tabloid — A small-sized newspaper (e.g. *The Sun*), which contains news but also a lot of gossip and celebrity stories.

Headline — The title of a main article (in a newspaper or magazine).

Strapline — An introductory headline, in a newspaper or magazine, just below a main headline.

Byline — The reporter's name, usually given under the headline.

Sub-heading — Headings used to break up the text into separate sections.

Cross-heads — Sub-headings within a block of text; these are often quotes.

Lead story — The main story on the front page of a newspaper or magazine.

Feature article — An article which covers a topic in some depth. A feature article is not usually about current news.

Human interest story — An article that focuses on a personal story, which is often sentimental.

Editorial — An opinion column which gives the newspaper's (or editor's) point of view on a subject or news story.

Columns — The layout of articles in newspapers and magazines – the text is usually laid out in a number of columns.

Caption — A few words or a short sentence which explains what a photo or picture shows.

Slogan — A catchy, memorable phrase often used in advertising.

Logo — A symbol or emblem unique to a product or company, used to represent that product or company.

Text box — A box containing text.

Font size — The size of the text.

Italic — A sloping font style: *italic*.

Helpful Hint

Using the terms listed on this page will help in your study of non-fiction and media texts, but don't just throw the words into your answers hoping to gain more marks.

DON'T just write, 'The writer uses cross-heads.' You must explain *why* the writer uses cross-heads.

DO write, 'The writer's use of cross-heads draws our attention to the article and arouses our curiosity so we are more likely to read beyond the headline.'

Language Techniques

When producing a piece of non-fiction or media writing, the writer considers the following:

- **Purpose:** why am I writing this piece?
- **Audience:** who am I writing this piece for?
- **Language:** what sort of language (style and tone) should I use? Formal / informal? Simple / technical?
- **Form:** where is the piece of writing going to appear? In a magazine or newspaper? On the Internet? In an advert? In a leaflet?

Purpose and Audience

First you need to work out what the text is trying to achieve (the purpose of the text) and who it is aimed at:

Does it contain descriptions of people, places or emotions?

Is the purpose of this to move the reader, recreate the past, gain the reader's sympathy etc.?

Does it contain argument or opinion?

Is the purpose of this to inform, persuade or change the reader's opinion?

Is it a narrative account (told as a sequence of events)?

Is the purpose of this to entertain, engage (i.e. make the reader feel involved), shock or move the reader?

Does it use contractions (e.g. we'll, 'don't) or full words?

Is this to target a young or old audience?

Does it contain 'masculine' or 'feminine' words (e.g. 'tough', 'blossom')?

Is this to target a male or female audience?

Form

Form refers to the way in which a text is presented. A text could be in the form of a letter, a book, a leaflet, an article in a newspaper or magazine, a web page etc. Different language techniques are used in different forms of writing, for example, a newspaper article is likely to use puns in its headlines.

Language

Style

Style refers to the overall effect created by…
* the type of words used
* the way in which words are used.

There are lots of different styles of language: it can be simple, using uncomplicated words and short sentences; it can be highly descriptive, using lots of adverbs and adjectives; it can be formal, using Standard English and an impersonal tone; it can be informal, using slang words and a structure that reflects spoken English, etc.

Tone

Tone refers to the mood, feeling or atmosphere created in a piece of writing. Different types of writing use different tones. For example, speeches by politicians have a passionate, personal tone to show that the speaker believes in what he / she is saying, whilst an article in a professional journal would probably have an impersonal, academic tone to sound factual and well researched.

The tone of a non-fiction or media text could be amusing / humorous, sarcastic, critical, factual, passionate, angry, serious, sad etc.

The style and tone of language a writer uses depends on the purpose of the writing and the audience (and, to an extent, the form).

The language influences the way the reader feels about the characters, ideas and events. In the exam, you need to show the examiner that you understand how the style and tone of writing affects your feelings when you read it.

The following are some basic style aspects that you should recognise when you are studying non-fiction or media texts in the exam.

Does the writer use the personal pronoun 'you' to address the reader?

This is called the direct address pronoun. It adds a personal touch and engages the reader (i.e. makes him / her feel involved). It sounds friendly, inviting and even confiding.

What narrative voice is used?

First person (I), second person (you), or third person (he, she, it, they)? Use of the first person gives an effect of the writer sharing an experience with the reader. This makes it sound more personal.

What use, if any, is made of dialogue?

Does the writer use direct speech (the exact words someone said, e.g. 'It was wonderful'), indirect speech (e.g. Mrs Jones said it was wonderful) or internal dialogue (when we are allowed to hear someone's thoughts and find out more about a particular character e.g. she stood there for some time thinking about how wonderful it all was).

What mood is created by language effects?

(e.g. reflective, lively, humorous or emotional)?

Are any connotations (hidden meanings) or associations linked with the words used?

Language Techniques

Media texts in particular often have a persuasive tone. Other texts may have an informative, argumentative, light-hearted tone, etc. Tone is created through the use of the following techniques.

Sensational and Emotive Language

Writers use language to be dramatic or to make the reader feel a particular emotion, e.g. excitement, sympathy or anger. Charity adverts are a good example of how a writer tries to manipulate a reader's feelings. They often use language to try to gain the reader's sympathy (and therefore persuade them to donate to the charity), for example...

> 'Poor Scamp was found starving, shivering and shaking in a cardboard box. He is still small for his age and needs constant medical attention.'

Exaggeration

Exaggeration is used to give greater emphasis to something. Writers often use exaggeration, especially when the purpose of the writing is to persuade or amuse. Exaggeration often includes the use of superlatives, for example, when the piece of writing states that something is the best, the greatest, the cleanest, the most effective, etc. Phrases from adverts are a good example of how writers use exaggeration to grab the reader's attention. For example...

> 'The most effective cleaner'
> 'The cheapest prices in town!'

Rhetorical Questions

A rhetorical question is a question which does not need an answer. The answer should be obvious from the text. Rhetorical questions are used for effect and to make the reader think. They are often used in newspaper articles, promotional leaflets, and adverts, for example...

> 'Thousands of cars are stolen every year. Is this kind of behaviour acceptable in our society?'

Alliteration

When words which are close together begin with the same sound it is called alliteration. Alliteration is used in pieces of writing to make a group of words stand out or to make something memorable. Alliteration is very often used in newspaper headlines, for example...

> 'Flash Flood Demolishes Farmhouse'
> 'House Prices Hit All Time High'

Use of Three

One of the easiest and most useful ways of emphasising a point is by using three words or phrases. Politicians often use this technique in speeches to stress an important point. Use of three is often found in media texts such as newspaper articles, for example...

> 'Restructuring the present system would be an expensive, time-consuming, and unworkable nightmare.'

Repetition

Sometimes a word or a group of words is repeated for emphasis. Repetition is often used in advertising, in newspaper articles, and in promotional leaflets. For example...

> 'Fact: More people than ever own several credit cards.
> Fact: More people than ever are in debt.'

Figures of Speech

A figure of speech is an expression which should not be taken literally. For example,

> 'It's raining cats and dogs' means it is raining heavily, not that animals are falling from the sky!

Make sure you know what the following terms mean, and that you are able to identify uses of them in non-fiction and media texts. You need to explain how these language features affect the reader's (your) feelings.

Simile

A simile compares one thing to another often using the words 'like' or 'as'. For example…

> 'Karen's hair shone like gold.'
> 'The bag was as light as a feather.'
> 'The thief moved through the garden like a stealthy cat.'

Metaphor

A metaphor describes one thing as if it were another. Do not confuse a metaphor with a simile. Metaphors never use 'like' or 'as'. For example…

> 'That car is a heap of old rubbish.'
> 'The fog was a grey veil over the city.'
> 'He is a cunning old fox.'

Imagery

Writers use imagery to paint a picture in the reader's mind and to help him / her relate to what is being described. If you notice use of imagery in the exam texts, make sure you say what kind of picture is created in your mind by the writer's choice of words.

Helpful Hint

Learn how to spell these language terms. The word 'simile' in particular is often spelt incorrectly.

If you are not sure whether you are writing about a simile or a metaphor, you can use the word 'imagery'. This is a general term for comparisons like similes and metaphors.

Analysing Language

Questions in this section of the exam will ask you to write about the way language is used in a non-fiction or media text. You need to consider the following three main points:

1. The words, phrases and language techniques that are used.
2. The effect they are intended to have on the reader.
3. How successful you think the writer has been in affecting / influencing the reader through language.

In order to answer a question on how the writer uses language, you should keep in mind a number of more detailed points. Here is a checklist:

- **What is the purpose of the text?**
  Is the text intended to argue, persuade, advise, inform, explain, describe, analyse, question, entertain or amuse?
- **What is the tone of the text?**
  Is it serious, light-hearted, formal, or informal?
- **Who is the intended audience?** (Remember to notice what kind of publication it comes from and what kind of people would read it.)
- **Is the text biased, impartial, personal, controversial, dramatic or emotional?**
- **How do you respond to the text?**
  Does it arouse any particular emotion in you?

- **Are there any language techniques used in the text?**
  Does it contain any similes, metaphors, imagery, alliteration etc.? If so, why have they been used?
- **Has the writer used a large number of adjectives to create a particular effect?**
- **Does the text address the reader directly by using the personal pronoun 'you'?**
- **Has the writer used persuasive language techniques** (e.g. repetition, use of threes, rhetorical questions, etc.)**?**
- **How successful do you think the writer has been in achieving his / her purpose?**

Helpful Hint

Remember to use evidence from the text, such as a short quote, to support your points. Do not simply write a list of general comments without providing examples to back them up.

Exam Preparation

Find two different non-fiction or media texts (e.g. a newspaper article and a leaflet) and study them. Write down some of the words and phrases that are used, why you think they have been used, and whether you think their use achieved the desired effect. Use the checklist on this page to help you.

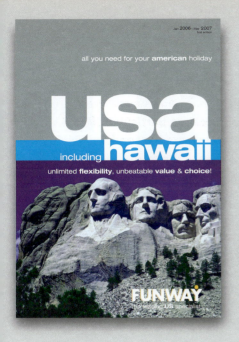

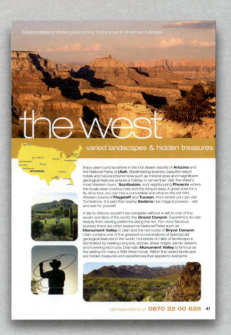

In a non-fiction text such as an autobiography, you may read something like this:

> 'I stood very still. I couldn't believe what I was seeing. How could he do this to me? My heart was ripped out in that split second and all I felt was shock. Pure shock.'

This text includes…

Short sentences: 'I stood very still'. These can make a point very effectively and put emphasis on something.

Rhetorical questions: 'How could he do this to me?' They are often used to engage and persuade the reader. They help to make a point in a more powerful and emotional way.

Metaphors: '…heart was ripped out…' Metaphors, similes, imagery and emotive language can be very effective and engaging. They can be used to make a scene vivid and to create mood and emotion.

Many media texts try to persuade you to do something. For example, adverts try to persuade you to buy particular products, and travel companies publish brochures to try to persuade you to visit specific places and to book one of their holidays. In a media text such as a travel brochure you may read something like this:

> 'An exceptional value holiday to Austria's Lake District, featuring spectacular scenery and superb sightseeing. With a lovely lakeside location and a host of included excursions, this really is a wonderful combination.'

This text includes…

Adjectives: describing words, such as 'spectacular' 'superb' and 'lovely'. These are used to convince the reader that the scenery is breathtaking, and adjective phrases such as 'an exceptional value holiday' and 'wonderful combination' suggest that the holiday is varied and well worth the money.

Alliteration: words next to each other which begin with the same letter, such as 'lovely lakeside location'. This is used to emphasise certain points, in this case, the attractive lakeside accommodation.

Other features to look out for are…

Description: this often contains imagery that can be very engaging.

Short anecdotes: writers use short anecdotes (short, personal stories which are often amusing) to add interest and engage the reader's attention. They are often used to introduce a piece of writing to grab the reader's attention.

Exaggeration: this is often used for effect (for example when trying to persuade or amuse).

Exam Preparation

Find one advert (in a newspaper or magazine) and one extract from a travel brochure. Highlight any adjectives and alliteration used in them, and say what these words add to the written piece.

Analysing Form and Presentation

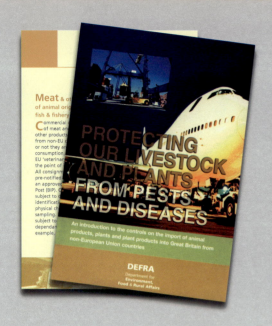

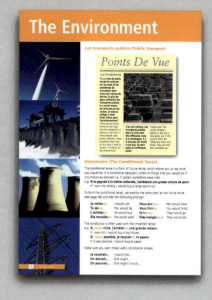

Form refers to how a text is presented and is closely linked to purpose. Newspapers, magazines, adverts etc. use a variety of devices to make an impact, including presentation, layout and images. In questions about form and presentation you need to consider these three main points:

1 The presentational devices that are used.
2 The effect they are intended to have on the reader.
3 How successful you think the presentational devices are in affecting / influencing the reader.

You need to show that you understand media concepts; you must show the examiner that you understand why various techniques have been used, such as why a magazine article contains a certain photo, or why a newspaper report is laid out in columns.

This checklist gives you an idea of what to look out for when answering questions about non-fiction and media texts and how they are presented.

- **Images, e.g. photographs, pictures, cartoons and diagrams:** analyse their position on the page and their appeal. What are they trying to achieve, and how successful are they?
- **Illustrations, e.g. graphs, maps and logos:** why have they been included? Are they informative or persuasive?
- **Image captions:** are they emotive, factual or humorous?
- **Colour:** is colour used at all in the text?
- **Headlines:** do the headlines contain alliteration or puns? Are they shocking or dramatic?

- **Sub-headings:** are they used to break up the text? Comment on their style and content. Do they focus on key issues in the text? Do they use alliteration or puns?
- **Font sizes:** are different sizes used for effect?
- **Upper case letters (capital letters):** are they used for key words etc.?
- **Bold type, italics or underlining:** do these appear anywhere in the text?
- **Catchy titles / headings and slogans:** these are often used in adverts.
- **Overall layout:** is the overall layout of the text eye-catching? Is the text divided up into columns? Is it divided up by pictures, sub-headings or bullet points? Or is it written in long paragraphs without any breaks?

Helpful Hint

Remember that it is not enough just to describe presentational features. You must analyse them. In other words, you must explain what effect they have on the reader and how or why this is so.

Exam Practice

Choose a magazine article that takes up one full page. Describe how the text is presented, why you think it is presented in this way and whether you think the presentation is successful. Use the checklist to help you.

Recognising Fact and Opinion

When you read non-fiction and media texts, you will come across both facts and opinions. You need to be able to distinguish between the two.

Facts are statements that we can prove; things we know for certain are true. Opinions are personal views. Some people will agree with them whereas others will not.

How to spot Opinion

Certain words signal opinion. The use of adjectives often signifies opinion rather than fact. Words such as seem, appear, suggest, might, may, should, could, would, supposedly, possibly, believe, apparently and allegedly, also imply opinion not fact.

Remember that writers often use exaggeration in order to persuade or to create a reaction in the reader. This often includes the use of superlatives (words such as 'best', 'greatest' 'nicest' etc., and the use of 'most …' as in 'most fantastic'). Superlatives often suggest someone's opinion.

Look at example 1 (below). Because a number has been used, you may think it is fact. Yet how do we know that the offers are 'fantastic'? This is just someone's opinion; other people might think they are far from 'fantastic'.

Look at example 2. This is fact because the statement can be checked and proved. It is not just someone's opinion.

Look at example 3, a shop sale sign. Not everyone will agree that the sale is the 'best ever' and no one will ever be able to prove this extravagant claim, which makes this text opinion, not fact.

Read example 4. The first two sentences are facts, as they can be checked and proven to be true. However, the final sentence is opinion. The adjectives 'worrying' and 'disgraceful' convey the writer's views rather than actual fact.

Helpful Hint

Adverts often contain outrageous claims about the products or services they are promoting. They tend to use opinion rather than fact to make the product /service seem better than it is.

Exam Preparation

Decide whether each of the following statements contain fact or opinion, and explain your answers.

* The most exciting theme park ride ever!
* All sale stock half-price!
* Tickets for the Madonna concert sold out within hours of going on sale.
* It could be her best tour to date.
* Open for business.

1
5 FANTASTIC OFFERS!

2
UP TO £500 OFF SELECTED MODELS

3
BEST EVER SALE!

4
Safety Assured

'When we test cars we always check the security of doors. In this report we reveal our findings. It adds up to a worrying picture for car owners and a disgraceful one for car manufacturers'.

Developing Your Answer

Remember that non-fiction texts are very varied. Many are biographies or autobiographies which focus on people's feelings about individuals or experiences they have had. Study this extract taken from Chapter 1 of William M. Thayer's biography *Abraham Lincoln*.

> The miserable log cabin in which Abraham Lincoln was born was a floorless, doorless, windowless shanty, situated in one of the most barren and desolate spots of Hardin County, Kentucky. His father made it his home simply because he was too poor to own a better one. Nor was his an exceptional case of penury and want. For the people of that section were generally poor and unlettered, barely able to scrape enough together to keep the wolf of hunger from their abodes.
>
> Here Abraham Lincoln was born February 12th, 1809. His father's name was Thomas Lincoln; his mother's maiden name was Nancy Hanks… They had been married three years when Abraham was born. Their cabin was in that part of Hardin County which is now embraced in La Rue County, a few miles from Hodgensville - on the south fork of Nolin Creek. A perennial spring of water, gushing in silvery brightness from beneath a rock near by, relieved the barrenness of the location, and won for it the somewhat ambitious name - "Rock Spring Farm."

Abraham Lincoln was President of the USA from 1861-1865.

Here is an example of the sort of question you could be asked on a non-fiction text like this one.

Q. How does Thayer use language to convey the place where Abraham Lincoln was born?

The following are some points you might decide to talk about in your answer to the question above.

- Negative phrases in the first paragraph suggest a difficult life in poor conditions, e.g. 'miserable log cabin', 'floorless…shanty'. These negative phrases emphasise Lincoln's humble start in life compared to him becoming President later in life and therefore having everything.
- Adjectives in the first paragraph help to create an image in the reader's mind of the poor living conditions Lincoln was born into, e.g. 'miserable', 'barren', 'desolate'.
- Use of three in 'floorless, doorless, windowless shanty' highlights the bad points of Lincoln's childhood home.
- Rhyme of 'floorless, doorless' makes these negative adjectives stand out.
- Metaphors, e.g. 'wolf of hunger'. This provides a vivid image of the fear of starvation.
- The second paragraph becomes more informative giving clear facts about Lincoln's parents.
- Phrases in the second paragraph are more positive than in the first, e.g. 'which is now embraced in…'. These positive words and phrases imply a happy life, despite the problems of where the family lived.
- Onomatopoeia is used, e.g. 'gushing', to highlight the fact that the water is the best thing about the location.
- The metaphor in the third paragraph is also more positive, e.g. 'gushing in silvery brightness'. This also suggests some beauty in the 'barrenness of the location'.

The Weekly News

Flash Floods Devastate Local Villages

Homes, businesses and lives ruined as flood water rises

Flash floods devastated villages in Derbyshire overnight on Friday. The full extent of the destruction is not yet known, but one thing is for certain: repairing the damaged property and getting people's lives back to normal could take months, if not years.

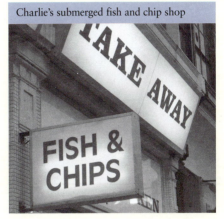

Charlie's submerged fish and chip shop

Destruction

One victim of the floods was Charlie Turner, 54, from Leafdale. He awoke on Saturday morning to find his home swamped under a metre of water. But there was more terrible news waiting for him in nearby Greenham when he went to open up the family business, Charlie's Chippie. He found flood water halfway up the walls and his deep-fat fryers completely submersed. Says Charlie, 'My grandfather Charlie opened this chippie in 1960 and we've been open 6 days a week ever since. I feel like I'm letting down the family name by having

to close up'. Charlie's life has been devastated by the flood and it will take him many months to repair the damage.

Widespread Damage

Every villager in Leafdale has a similar story to tell, and although the weather is due to ease this week, this is no consolation to the many whose homes and businesses have already been ruined. Single mum-of-two Anna Grayson said, 'I just don't know where to start. We're going to have to stay at my mum's until the repair work can be done on the house. It's just a dreadful situation'.

Many media texts try to persuade the audience or try to gain their sympathy by using various persuasive techniques and other language devices. Study the newspaper article above.

Here is an example of the sort of question you could be asked on a media text like this one in the exam.

Q. How is language used in this article to gain sympathy from its readers?

The following are some points you might decide to talk about in your answer to the question above.

- The headline uses alliteration in 'flash floods' to highlight the main point of the article. The use of the word 'flash' also implies that it happened so quickly the villagers weren't prepared for it.
- Use of three in the strapline ('Homes, businesses and lives') emphasises the damage caused by the flood.
- Sensational words are used throughout the article for effect, e.g. 'destruction', 'terrible', 'devasted'.

- Emotive words are used in the article, for example, 'victim'.
- The fact that the article uses quotes from people who have been affected by the flood makes it seem more real, and allows the reader to identify with the situation the people face.
- The article focuses in particular on one 'victim of the floods' whose home and business have been damaged. This highlights the extent of the flood damage. A quote from this man is used, which talks about how long his business has been going and how it was founded by his grandfather. This gains sympathy by stressing the family connection.
- Use of 'single mum-of-two' lets readers identify and sympathise with the woman's situation.
- Opinion is used by the writer to sound like fact, e.g. 'repairing the damaged property... could take months'. This again highlights the extent of the damage and suggests that the people will suffer for a long time.

Exam Tips

In order to perform at your best in the exam, you need to be in control of your whole approach to it.

Before the exam, make sure that you…

- learn the key points covered in this section of the guide
- know the kind of questions you are likely to get
- practise writing within the time limits of the exam. Try to work through as many past papers as possible (have a go at the exam practice questions on the next page)
- check carefully the exact dates and times of your exams
- give yourself plenty of time to get to the exam. You should arrive at least 30 minutes before the exam starts so that you can prepare yourself calmly.

In the exam, make sure that you…

- read the instructions on the paper carefully
- work out how long you should spend on each question according to how many marks are available
- read the questions carefully and plan your answers before you start writing
- follow the bullet points given in the question – they are there to help you
- use accurate spelling, punctuation and grammar
- use Standard English, not slang or the kind of language you use with your friends
- remember to analyse: think about 'how' and 'why' rather than 'what'. (This means think about explaining how language and presentational techniques are used and why they are used, rather than just saying what is used.)
- use the PEE technique (Point, Evidence, Explanation).

Useful Phrases

The following are phrases which you may find useful when writing your answers in the exam.

- It seems the writer wants to persuade the reader that…
- The views expressed in these articles are quite different. We realise this immediately from…
- Both texts begin by mentioning that…
- The headline of the article is very effective because…
- The layout of the advertisement catches the reader's eye because…

Exam Practice

Ask your teacher for past exam papers. Have a good look at them so that you are familiar with the layout and work through as many questions as possible to prepare for the exam.

Weight Loss
The Fact and the Fantasy

We all want to lose a little weight this New Year, and we may all think that we know how. Many given 'facts' about weight loss, however, are complete horse feathers...

Fantasy

Diets really work for permanent weight loss

Fact

Most diets are codswallop; those that do work should really only be used to kickstart a healthy, long-term eating plan. Any diet that seriously restricts your calorie intake or limits the number of foods you can eat is extremely difficult to stick to; if you then go back to eating normally you will simply regain the weight. Avoid diets like the Atkins plan; diets like this do not give you all the nutrients your body needs and will only result in health problems. Much better is to get into a balanced, healthy eating habit.

Fantasy

If I want to lose weight I must cut my favourite sweet or fatty foods out of my diet.

Fact

That's not strictly true. In order to lose weight you must be burning more calories than you are eating; while sweet or fatty foods are generally higher in calories than healthier options, provided your calories intake remains lower than your body's minimum energy requirement you can eat whatever you like. After all, a pattern of eating with absolutely no treats at all would be a very grim existence – and who wants to be thin and miserable?

Fantasy

Skipping meals will help me to lose weight.

Fact

Again, complete bunkum. Obviously, not eating at all will lower your calorie intake, but this is the silliest way to do it. Further more studies show that people who eat smaller portions more often find it easier to lose weight, because they are much better at managing their appetites.

Fantasy

Eating after 8pm will make me put on weight.

Fact

Weight loss / gain depends on the balance between your daily intake of calories and your daily energy requirement (of course, this requirement is higher the more physical activity you do, so figure your exercise into the equation). What time of day you eat has no effect at all – your body will store surplus calories as fat either way.

Fantasy

Natural or herbal weight-loss products are safe and effective.

Fact

There is no easy way to lose weight, unfortunately. Weight-loss products can help, but even products claiming to be 'natural' can be dangerous, since they are rarely rigorously tested and can have serious side effects on your body. Lose weight in the way that is 100% natural: eat fresh, healthy food and push it through your body with some exhilarating exercise – you'll soon see and feel the difference. Fact!

Read the advert and the article on this page.

1. What are the key points in the 'Weight Loss' article?
2. What are the key points in the 'Fat Combat' advert?
3. Compare the way language is used in both the texts.
4. How effective is the presentation of the advert and the article? Comment on:
   - what you think the designers of the texts set out to do
   - the way the material is set out in each text
   - the use of presentational devices.

Don't lose £s, lose lbs!

FAT COMBAT

FREE REASONS TO JOIN!

- Free personal consultation
- Free weekly newsletter
- Free weight loss plan – individually tailored to suit you.

CHOOSE TO LOSE!

"Fat Combat changed my life! I dropped two dress sizes in a month".
Carolyn, 29

Join before June 30th and enjoy
3 MONTHS' FREE MEMBERSHIP*

* Usually £35 per month

Writing to Argue, Persuade or Advise

The Exam Question

In Section B of Paper 1, you will be tested on your ability to write. You will have a choice of four questions; each question will ask you to produce a different kind of writing. You will have 45 minutes to complete **one** question of your choice. You should spend ten minutes of this time planning and checking your answer. The questions will cover three different types of writing:

- writing to argue
- writing to persuade
- writing to advise.

The choice of questions usually includes one for each type of writing and a further question which combines two of the three types (for example, argue and persuade).

What is the examiner looking for?

The examiner wants to know that you can write accurately and appropriately in English. Regardless of which question you choose to answer the examiner will always be looking for the same things. Many of the marking criteria are the same as for Section B of Paper 2 (writing to inform, explain or describe - see page 74). You need to make sure that you are able to do the following:

- Communicate and express your ideas clearly in writing.
- Organise ideas into sentences, paragraphs and whole texts, and try to use a variety of sentence structures.
- Punctuate accurately with commas, full stops, apostrophes etc.
- Spell words correctly.
- Use a wide vocabulary: don't just use the first or most basic word you think of. Try to use a word that really portrays what you want to say.
- Write in different forms effectively (e.g. letters, leaflets).
- Use Standard English – do not use 'text' language (e.g. 'u' instead of 'you') except where appropriate or requested.
- Make the purpose of your writing clear.
- Write for a particular audience.
- Present your work clearly in neat handwriting so that the examiner can easily read and understand your answer.

Left column examples

Writing to Argue

96 Oak Close
Southampton

Daily News
Main Street
Southampton

Dear Editor

I read with horror yesterday your article on banning ball games in Wentworth Park. I believe this campaign against ball games is totally wrong.

With rising obesity levels amongst young people I believe we should encourage people to play more sport.

Some people may argue that ball games are dangerous. But young people have always played in the park and I believe they still should.

Yours faithfully

D. Jeffries

Mrs D Jeffries

Writing to Persuade

PGFCA

Scrappy was starving when we found her and Pip had been wandering the streets for weeks surviving anyway she could.

Many animals do not have anyone to love them. Could that person be you? For only £2 per month you could say 'I love you' to an abandoned animal.

Writing to Advise

exams & revision
ADVICE

If you want to get top grades then a revision plan is essential.

• Make a revision timetable that you can stick to.
• Get past papers or questions from your teachers.
• Find a quiet place to study where you won't be disturbed.
• Find your revison style – our quick quiz on page 3 will help you.
• Revise in short bursts.

Writing to Argue

Arguing involves expressing a point of view as clearly and effectively as possible. This will usually include presenting evidence and a series of reasons for your argument. You must...

• express a point of view
• be aware that someone else has a different point of view
• try to achieve a balanced argument. Don't just put forward your view.

The letter opposite, written to a newspaper, is an example of writing to argue.

Writing to Persuade

Persuading involves getting your readers to agree with a point of view or making them feel a certain way. This might involve argument, but it will usually also involve other methods of trying to influence people's feelings. You must...

• try to make someone do something they might not want to do
• understand why they might not want to do this
• use different techniques to try to persuade them.

The charity advert opposite is an example of writing to persuade.

Writing to Advise

Advising involves giving someone help by telling them as clearly as possible how to do something. You must...

• write in a personal, persuasive way
• write in role as a person who knows the answers.

The extract opposite, from a leaflet about exams and revision, is an example of writing to advise.

There may be elements of other types of writing in your chosen question as well as the one specified; for example, in order to write a letter persuading somebody to agree with you on an issue, you may need to include your argument for the issue. Always make sure you focus on the type of writing that appears in bold print in the question; this is the type of writing the question is testing you on.

Purpose, Audience, Form and Language

Purpose and Audience

The first things you need to know when starting to write are…

- **What is the purpose of the writing?**
  What are you trying to achieve through the writing?
- **Who is your audience?**
  Who are you writing for? Do you know the person? How old is he / she?

We know that the purpose of the writing in this section of the exam is to argue, persuade or advise (or a combination of them). You may be asked to…

- argue for or against something
- persuade someone to do or not to do something
- advise someone on the best, easiest, quickest or most effective way to do something.

There are many possibilities of audience you may be asked to write to / for. Here are some examples of possible audiences (there are many more):

- Teenagers
- Adults
- Children
- Football fans
- The local council
- Pupils at your school
- Teachers

Helpful Hint

If the question you choose to answer does not state a specific audience, write as you would when you write an essay; keep your language quite formal and avoid using the personal pronoun 'you' too much, as you cannot address your audience directly when you don't know who they are. See page 83.

Form

Every piece of writing has a particular form. The form is how the writing is presented. In this section of the exam, you are often asked to write in a particular form. Here are some examples of forms that you could be asked to write in:

- Holiday brochure extracts
- Newspaper reports
- Magazine articles
- Informal or formal letters
- Leaflets
- Advice sheets
- News sheets
- Memos
- On-line pages / emails

Language

The language you use in your writing should be appropriate for the audience you are aiming at so you need to make sure you adopt the right register (tone). Register is the tone of voice and the level of formality you use when speaking and writing. You wouldn't speak to your teachers in the same way you speak to your brothers and sisters, so the register needs to be chosen carefully. The audience is the main thing that influences your choice of register, however, the purpose and form will also affect the type of language you use.

Here is a good mnemonic (way to help you memorise) which is easy to learn and will help you to remember the main points to consider when answering the exam question:

F - Form
L - Language and register
A - Audience
P - Purpose

For example, imagine there is a huge party on Friday night. But there is one big problem - it is during your exams and your teacher is sending letters home telling everyone they must stay in and revise.

Q. Write a letter to your teacher **persuading** her to let you go to the party.

What form, language, audience and purpose are needed for this piece of writing? Start by underlining the clues that are in the question. (The purpose, e.g. persuade, will be printed in bold in the exam paper.) Your question would then look something like this…

Q. 'Write a <u>letter</u> to your <u>teacher</u> **persuading** her to let you go to the party.'

So now you have the form, audience and purpose. The form, audience and purpose tell you which type of language to use so if you are using the FLAP mnemonic to help you, fill in the language section last.

Form   - letter
Language - formal (it's to your teacher, not your best friend!)
Audience - your teacher
Purpose   - persuade

Exam Preparation

Underline the key words in the following question and then use the FLAP technique to identify the form, language, audience and purpose.

Q. Write a speech to be made at a governors' meeting where you, as a student, try to **persuade** governors to abolish school uniform.

Once you have chosen which question you are going to answer in the exam, and you know the audience, purpose, form and language (register), the next stage is planning your answer.

Planning Your Answer

In your exam you should spend about five minutes planning your answer. You won't get any extra marks for planning but it will help you to write organised and well-structured pieces which will, in turn, help you to get a higher grade. A plan will ensure that you discuss every subject you want to cover in a logical, sensible order; this will make your piece of writing better.

There are a number of ways to plan your answer; the most common techniques are shown here as responses to the following question:

Q. Write a letter to the school governors to try to **persuade** them to abolish school uniform.

1 Brainstorm

Brainstorming your ideas or using a 'mind map' is an easy but effective way to plan.

Paragraph 1
Why uniform is bad
- Everyone looks the same
- Ties are dangerous
- Uncomfortable

Paragraph 2
Why uniform is good
- Looks tidy
- Poorer pupils can afford it
- Makes you feel part of school

LETTER TO GOVERNORS

Paragraph 3
Why the above is wrong
- Everyone tries to make it look different
- Everyone still knows who the poor kids are
- Shouldn't need uniform to make you feel like you belong

Conclusion
- Europe doesn't have uniform
- This is the 21st century – people can be more individual

2 A List

A list is a simple and clear way to plan what you are going to say.

LETTER TO GOVERNORS

Paragraph 1: Uniform is bad

- Everyone looks the same
- Ties are dangerous
- Uncomfortable

Paragraph 2: Uniform is good

- Looks tidy
- Poorer pupils can afford it
- Makes you feel part of school

Paragraph 3: Why the above is wrong

- Everyone tries to make it look different
- Still know who the poor kids are
- Shouldn't need uniform to make you feel like you belong

Conclusion

- Europe doesn't have uniform
- This is the 21st century – people can be more individual

3   A Writing Frame

Many students find writing frames helpful. They are just another way of organising your thoughts using key phrases in each section. So, for your introduction in a letter you may write something like 'I am writing to you today…'.

	Date
Address	

Dear

On behalf of the school council, I am writing…

We feel very strongly about this issue.

Although I recognise that there are some arguments against my proposals…

However I feel that…

I hope therefore that you can offer your support…

Yours…

Exam Preparation

Read the following question and make a plan in one of the three ways shown here. You could try making a plan in each of the three ways shown to decide which technique works best for you.

Q. Write a letter to a local newspaper in which you **argue** that the council needs to provide more recycling facilities in the local area.

Helpful Hints

Give yourself about five minutes in the exam to plan your answer, but don't take much longer than this; the plan will not count towards your mark so make sure you spend enough time actually writing your answer.

You don't have to stick rigidly to your plan. If you find whilst you are writing your answer that you want to add something, leave something out, or swap the order around, straying slightly from the plan won't affect your mark.

It doesn't matter which technique you use to plan your answer, as long as you plan.

Language: Connectives

When you are writing to argue, persuade or advise there are certain language techniques that you can use to help structure your argument, your persuasive piece or your advice. One important language technique is the use of connectives (also known as discourse markers). Connectives are words and phrases that link paragraphs, sentences, or clauses within sentences (e.g. although, because, and). (See page 94 for more information.) You can use them in the following ways:

1 As connectors at the beginning of a sentence, for example, '**Naturally**, some people will say that we should be free to decide our own future'.

2 As connectors in the middle of a sentence, for example, 'Caving in winter is dangerous **because** the caves can quickly fill with water'.

3 To connect your paragraphs, for example, 'We believe that forcing students to wear an uncomfortable uniform is wrong.

    Obviously, I realise that some people feel differently about uniform'.

Connectives in Writing to Argue

Connectives can be particularly useful when you are writing to argue for or against something. They can be used very effectively to open and close an argument. For example,

- **Firstly**, I would like to note that…
- **Clearly**, we are living in dangerous times…
- **In conclusion**, I feel that…

Connectives in Writing to Persuade or Advise

Connectives can be useful in writing to persuade or advise because they allow you to state the issue and then connect it naturally to the subject you are trying to persuade or advise the audience on. For example,

- This can be a problem. **Therefore**, I felt it would help you to…
- This may be quite stressful. **So**, I thought you may like to…
- I don't mean to bother you **but**…

Here is a list of some of the more commonly used connectives. It may help you to learn some of these connectives so that you can use them effectively in the exam.

First of all	As
Most importantly	Equally
In addition	Finally
Nevertheless	Even so
Therefore	For example
However	Although

Exam Preparation

Using the connectives given on this page, write a letter to a newspaper summarising your argument about an issue you feel strongly about (e.g. the environment, smoking).

- Try and write your argument in roughly 200 words. (This is less than you will need to write in the exam.)
- Try to use at least one connective in all of the following places:
  - to open a sentence
  - to connect a sentence
  - to open a paragraph
  - in your introduction
  - in your conclusion.

Structure and Form: Paragraphs

The examiner will be looking for evidence of paragraphs when marking your writing paper. Paragraphs are used to organise pieces of writing. A paragraph is a set of sentences which have related ideas or subjects. Paragraphs are usually shown in one of two ways:

1 By leaving a line before starting a new paragraph:

> We believe that forcing students to wear an uncomfortable and dangerous uniform is wrong.
>
> I realise that some people feel differently about uniform and believe its benefits outweigh its negative points.

2 By indenting the text when you start a new paragraph:

> We believe that forcing students to wear an uncomfortable and dangerous uniform is wrong.
>
>   I realise that some people feel differently about uniform and believe its benefits outweigh its negative points.

Helpful Hint

If, at the end of the exam, you realise you have forgotten to use paragraphs, mark where you would separate the paragraphs by inserting a slash where each paragraph break should be, e.g.

> We believe that forcing students to wear an uncomfortable uniform is wrong. / I realise that some people feel differently about uniform and believe it has many benefits.

You could also write 'NP' (new paragraph) in the margin, e.g.

> We believe that forcing students to wear an
> **NP** uncomfortable uniform is wrong. / I realise that some people feel differently about uniform and believe it has many benefits.

Try not to do this in all your answers - it is not a replacement for paragraphs and will show the examiner that you haven't planned your answers.

When to Start a New Paragraph

Paragraphs are used to break up the text into groups of sentences. Using paragraphs means you don't end up with a solid block of text, and it allows you to present your writing in an organised way so that your ideas are easier to follow. A new paragraph is used when you have any of the following:

- **A change of time**, for example,

> During the summer holidays, Sarah decided to go to work at the animal sanctuary. The summer holidays were very long and Sarah loved being outdoors with the animals.
>
> When winter came with its dark nights, Sarah hated being outside.

- **A change of speaker**, for example,

> "Maybe we should have stayed," said Fern, "What if they notice we're missing?"
>
> "We'll get into trouble," said Rafferty.

- **A change of place or person**, for example,

> The hills surrounding the village are dominated by ten large wind turbines.
>
> The wooded valley, two miles from the village, is protected.

Structure and Form: Paragraphs

Beginning and Ending

Every piece of writing should have an opening paragraph and a closing (concluding) paragraph. Examiners want to see that you have thought about the structure of your writing carefully so that the opening makes your intentions clear, and the conclusion summarises the main points.

A good opening paragraph in writing to persuade might flatter or compliment the reader to gain their interest. A good opening paragraph in writing to advise might offer a compliment or a sympathetic phrase to the reader to gain their trust and confidence.

Look at the example opposite of a good opening paragraph for writing to persuade.

In this example the writer gains the reader's attention and trust by complimenting his / her home and empathising with him / her. The writer then hints at the purpose of the writing with a rhetorical question to introduce what follows.

A good opening paragraph in writing to argue will describe your intentions and views whilst recognising others.

Look at the example opposite of a good opening paragraph for writing to argue.

In this example the writer states his / her view clearly, and recognises the opposing point.

A good conclusion to any piece of writing will summarise the main points you have made in your writing.

Look at the example opposite of a good concluding paragraph to the letter.

In this example the writer opens the final paragraph well with the use of 'In conclusion', and goes on to summarise the main points of the letter, including the opposing viewpoint. The writer rounds the letter off well by suggesting that she expects a response.

Writing to Persuade

Your home is your haven, your favourite place to be - a special place for you, your family and your memories. Why not make it even more special by extending with a beautiful classic conservatory?

Writing to Argue

96 Oak Close,
Southampton.

Daily News,
1 Main Street,
Southampton

Dear Sir / Madam

I am writing to you to voice my opposition to the building of a supermarket on the recreation ground in the village. Whilst I am strongly against this proposal I do recognise that there are some equally important issues about the lack of a supermarket in the village that need addressing.

cont...

A conclusion

In conclusion I feel I have shown that the recreation ground is vital to the village in many ways and, whilst the problems of the elderly and access to supermarkets do need addressing, I feel that this cannot be at the expense of village life. I hope you take my proposals on board and I look forward to hearing from you in the future.

Yours faithfully

D Jeffries

Mrs D Jeffries

Structure and Form: Articles

In this section of the exam, it is likely that you will get a question asking you to write an article for a newspaper, magazine or an Internet website. This may be to argue a point, persuade the readers on an issue, or advise readers on a subject. You may get a question such as this:

Q. Write an article for a health magazine in which you give **advice** to university students on how to stay fit and healthy on a budget.

Features of Articles

Newspapers and magazines use a variety of techniques to grab the reader's attention; this includes the structure of the article, and the language used in it.

Each article has a **headline** which summarises the content of the article or picks out a particular feature of the article designed to intrigue, shock or amuse the reader.

The main or longer articles also have a **strapline** which further explains what the story is about and draws attention to its main points.

Sub-headings are also used in articles to separate the text, particularly in long articles, where they may appear as headings to certain paragraphs.

The following language techniques are frequently used in newspaper headlines and sub-headings to grab the reader's attention:

- **Emotive language** e.g. 'Drunken beast fined £500'
- **Sensational (dramatic) language** e.g. 'Road of Death'

- **Pun / Play on words** e.g. 'She's parking mad!'
- **Rhetorical questions:** questions where the answer is obvious, and therefore isn't required, e.g. 'Would you want to live like this?'
- **Rhyme** e.g. 'Andy the bin man's greatest fan'
- **Alliteration:** repetition of the first letter of two or more words in a sentence, e.g. 'Clifford the cat calls 999'.

Content

Newspaper articles often include direct quotes or reported speech from victims, experts, eyewitnesses etc. Often this will just include their name, age and occupation or relevance to the story, for example,
   'Joe Smith, 23, who lived next door, said...'.
This is known as non-essential information: information that isn't essential to the story but adds more detail and interest to it.

Style

Reports are generally written in the past tense (e.g. 'He went...', ' It was...', 'They drove off...') as the article is a report on something that has already happened. Of course, there are exceptions, for example, a local newspaper might run an article about a forthcoming Christmas fair, including what will be there, when and where it will take place etc. But even these types of articles may also use the past tense, for example, in referring to last year's Christmas fair.

Note that headlines often use the present tense, e.g. 'Clifford the cat calls 999.'

Structure and Form: Articles

Structure of Articles

The first paragraph in a newspaper or magazine article should be fairly short; it should contain 25 words or less and may be just one or two sentences. Often the first paragraph in a newspaper article appears in a larger font size than the rest and in bold. It must include who, what, where and when (who the story is about, what happened, where it took place and when it took place). For example,

> 'Yesterday, in Verona, a bloody battle raged between the two feuding families, the Capulets and the Montagues.'

When	Where	What	Who

The second paragraph in the article usually develops the brief information given in the first paragraph, using more detail.

The third and following paragraphs should give additional information and look at why the incident/event happened and how.

So remember...

- Headline: try to use one of the language devices listed on page 37.
- First paragraph: should be 25 words or less and include: who, what, where and when.
- Second paragraph: should relate to your first paragraph but give more detail.
- Third and following paragraphs: should give additional information and look at why and how.
- Don't forget eye witness reports and expert opinions.

Exam Preparation

Read the following statement taken from a school girl who witnessed an assault. Using the information on this page, put the details into the order in which they would appear in a newspaper article.

1. Headline
2. First paragraph
3. Second paragraph
4. Third and following paragraphs

> There is this stupid gang of ex-students who hang around the school gates. They have nothing else to do. Matt Jones is their leader; he's only 17 but is always drunk and gets into a lot of trouble around town. His girlfriend is in Year 10. She went to this party last Friday with Peter Smith. Anyway, Peter came out of school and Matt went for him and hit him over the head with a bottle. There was blood everywhere. Matt's friends were laughing and no one knew what to do. Then the lollipop lady, Mrs Green, came running over and told Matt off and helped Peter. Matt was swearing at her but she ignored him and called the police. Matt ran off but the police have arrested him.

See page 80 for more on writing articles.

Emotive and Sensational Language

Newspaper and magazine articles are often full of emotive and sensational language. Emotive language is used to try to influence your emotions (feelings). Sensational language is dramatic language which is used to make a piece of writing more exciting, more vivid or more engrossing. Emotive and sensational language are used a lot in many types of writing, particularly in writing to argue and writing to persuade.

Look at the newspaper article below. It uses emotive and sensational language to persuade the reader that the attacker is an evil beast and the victim is a gentle, loving father.

The headline

- 'Beast' is the first word of the article and it suggests something horrible; it is something we think we would not like. Before we have had any information about the story, we already dislike the person involved. This is an example of emotive language.
- 'Battered' is a very harsh, negative word which is quite sensational. Why didn't the writer just use the word 'hit' here?

- 'Best pal' is emotive in a positive sense – we feel sympathy towards the victim because he was his best friend, and therefore trusted his attacker.
- 'Beast', 'battered' and 'best' have an alliterative effect. Alliteration is often used in headlines.

The strapline

- 'Drunken devil' is alliterative and emotive. No one likes a devil, especially not a drunken one.
- 'Stunned' is sensational. Why didn't the writer just use the word 'upset'?

The first paragraph

- 'Sozzled Sykes' has an alliterative effect and emphasises how drunk the attacker was.
- 'Dad-of-two' is emotive language, used to gain more sympathy for the victim.

Exam Preparation

Write a strapline and the first three paragraphs of a newspaper article based on the headline 'Man found alive after missing for two years'. Use the advice given here and try to include emotive and sensational language, alliteration, rhyme and puns.

The Lonsdale News, Tuesday, January 17, 2006   12

BEAST WHO BATTERED BEST PAL GETS OFF WITH CAUTION

Drunken devil John Sykes, 29, stunned people in a local park by battering best friend Brian Jones.

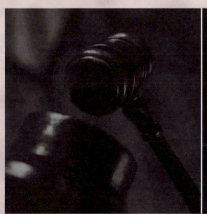

The two were heading home from a local pub on Friday night when sozzled Sykes turned on dad-of two Jones, 25.

Horrified passers-by were shocked when the 22-stone builder suddenly took a swing at Jones, beating him black and blue, before spinelessly staggering off.

Structure and Form: Leaflets

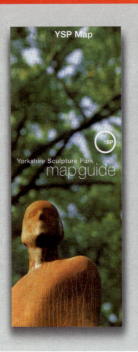

In this section of the exam it is possible that you may be asked to write the text for a leaflet or information sheet. (See page 81 for more on leaflets.) This is usually to persuade or advise. They will cover all the devices used to argue, persuade or advise covered in this chapter. You may get a question such as this:

Q. Write the text for a leaflet written by an environmental group who focus on the need to recycle. Try to **persuade** teenagers to join this environmental group.

Leaflets usually contain a mixture of facts and opinions. A fact is something that can be proven to be true. An opinion is someone's viewpoint. (See page 23.)

Techniques for Writing Leaflets

- Plan your leaflet with your audience in mind.
- Create an effective headline.
- Your first paragraph should catch the reader's attention.
- Sub-headings can guide the reader through the text and lead them to important points.
- Bullet points and text boxes are often used in leaflets, but remember this is an English writing exam – you won't get full marks if you only use bullet points.
- Use a mixture of fact and opinion.

Presentational Devices

You will not be expected to spend time on presentational devices, other than simple headings

and sub-headings (and perhaps bullet points or a numbered list). Do not waste time on drawings.

A leaflet is often a sheet of A4 paper that has been folded to make it more noticeable / interesting. In the exam you are not expected to fold your leaflet. Folding your answer paper may confuse the examiner and could make your writing more difficult to follow.

Some students confuse columns with paragraphs. Remember that a column is a vertical presentational device whereas a paragraph is a horizontal organisational device. Do not write in columns – again this could make your work difficult to follow.

Helpful Hint

Remember that the examiner wants to see that you can write well in English, not that you can make your answer paper look like a real leaflet.

Exam Preparation

Make a list of the techniques you could use when writing a leaflet to persuade young people to stop smoking. The list has been started for you. Try to think of another five language techniques you could use, and give an example for each. (Use pages 6 and 7 to help you if you get stuck.)

1. Emotive language, e.g. 'If you carry on smoking you will die'.
2. Metaphors, e.g. 'A cigarette is cancer in a stick'.

Structure and Form: Speech Writing

Speeches are good examples of writing to persuade and writing to argue. For example, a political speech is written to try to persuade the audience to vote for that party. There are many techniques used by speech writers to hold the audience's interest and to try to influence their views. You may get a question such as this:

Q. Write the text for a speech where you **argue** the case for free university education for all.

Like any piece of writing, speeches should be organised into clear paragraphs. They should contain language which grabs the audience's attention. However, speeches are written to be read out loud so you need to use language devices that can be heard.

Language Devices for Speeches

- **Use of three** is frequently used in speeches. It may be three questions, three rhetorical questions, three points etc. Use of three is very good at emphasising a point and is very effective when spoken aloud, e.g. 'I came, I saw, I conquered'.
- **Repetition** emphasises words and phrases and makes them stick in the listener's mind.
- **Parallelism** involves the repetition of sentences with similar structures, e.g. 'It was the best of times; it was the worst of times'.
- **Contrasts and opposites** are used in speeches for emphasis by putting one word or idea next to a different word or idea, e.g. 'Arise fair sun and kill the envious moon'. This contrasts the sun with the moon, and life with death. Opposites work in the same way, e.g. 'It's a matter of life and death'.
- **Rhetorical questions** are great for speeches as they address the listeners in a way that makes them feel involved.
- **Use of personal pronouns** (I, me, you, he, him, she, her, it, we, us, they, them), possessive pronouns (our, my), and friendly terms of address (e.g. 'Comrades', 'Friends') breaks down barriers between the speaker and the audience, making the audience feel more involved. The use of 'I' also indicates the speaker's authority.

- **Emotive and sensational language** in a speech can make the audience feel a certain way, e.g. sympathetic or shocked.
- **Lists:** listing subjects, items, names etc. can emphasise how many / few there are of something, e.g. listing the countries where millions live in poverty highlights the extent of the problem.

Exam Practice

Look at the following speech given by a student about abolishing school uniform.

> My fellow students, friends, I am delighted to have the opportunity to speak with you today.
>
> There are many wonderful things about our school, but the uniform is not one of them. Do you want to keep wearing this awful uniform? Do you want to look the same as everyone else? Do you want to wear uncomfortable clothes? I say it is time to stop the old-fashioned and out-of-date practices; I say it is time for us as students to say no to this dreadful uniform; I say it is time the teachers and the governors listened to the students' voices. I say it is time to abolish this uniform and let freedom of expression reign.
>
> The uniform that we are forced to wear every lesson, every day, every year is out-of-date, ugly and expensive.

Which speech writing devices has the student used? Could this speech be improved upon? Write your own speech arguing for school uniform to be abolished.

Writing to Argue

Writing an argument means expressing your opinion - what you think and feel about an issue.

It sounds simple but in order to achieve a good grade you also need to be aware that someone else has a different point of view, and try to achieve a balanced argument.

Structuring your Argument

1 **Introduction:** this should clearly state your opinion.

2 **Main body:** this will include...
- Your argument (to back up your opinion)
- An acknowledgement of the other argument / opinion
- Counter argument (why you believe the other person's view is wrong. You have to try and guess what they might say and then argue against that point of view).
- Evidence

3 **Conclusion:** this should summarise your argument.

Techniques in Writing to Argue

Here are some techniques you could use to make your argument as convincing as possible:

- A **positive opening** that clearly states your opinion.
- **Connectives...**
  - to give your piece structure, e.g. firstly, secondly.
  - to express cause and effect, e.g. consequently.
  - to express comparisons to link your arguments, e.g. however, on the other hand.
- **Present tense** to make your argument seem more immediate.
- **Personal Pronouns** to give a personal tone and make your argument seem more believable.
- **Rhetorical questions** to highlight the issue and involve the reader.
- **PEE technique (Point, Evidence, Explanation,** see page 14) to introduce evidence.
- A series of **paragraphs** that give argument and counter argument.
- **Comparative devices** such as similes and metaphors to emphasise your main points.
- **Conclusion** to summarise and re-state your opinion.

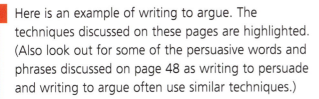

Here is an example of writing to argue. The techniques discussed on these pages are highlighted. (Also look out for some of the persuasive words and phrases discussed on page 48 as writing to persuade and writing to argue often use similar techniques.)

page 48

Exam Practice

Write an article for a teenagers' magazine in which you **argue** against people wearing clothes and accessories made out of real animal fur. You could talk about…

- why wearing real fur is wrong
- what alternative is available.

Use of 'I' and present tense makes argument seem believable

Opinion clearly stated

Point
Evidence
Explanation

Giving an alternative view

Polite but convincing

Connective used to help structure the argument

Rhetorical questions used to involve the reader

Use of three

Discrediting the other opinion

Rhetorical questions used to discredit the other opinion

Exclamations in the form of imperatives (commands) are used to emphasise the point

Conclusion summarises opinion

Metaphor to stress the point

Dear Students,

I am writing to you today to give you my views on smoking. This is an expensive addiction which is bad for your health.

Smoking destroys your heart and lungs, makes you look old and could kill you. The law tries to protect young people from smoking by making the legal age for buying cigarettes 16; they do this because they know that smoking has a terrible effect on people's lives. I believe that it is school's job to protect young people too.

Some young people believe it is their right to smoke, that they have freedom of choice, especially once they are 16. I am sure you will agree that these arguments are foolish.

Firstly, most children who smoke in school are not 16 and, even if they were, the local education authority has banned smoking in all schools so no-one has the right to smoke in schools.

Secondly, we all know the harm that passive smoking can do. What right have these people to make us breathe in their second-hand smoke whilst travelling on the bus or using the toilets?

Some younger members of the school are afraid to go to the toilets because of the smokers. Is this right? Is this fair?

At school we are starting a Shout Out! campaign against smokers. There are three things we plan to do: have more teacher patrols in the toilets; have stricter sanctions against people caught smoking, and encourage you to shout out and let us know who is smoking.

Some people may call this snitching or grassing and say it is wrong to tell on the smokers. Clearly this is not true. We must tell on smokers; not only are they breaking the law but as we all know, passive smoking can be just as dangerous as smoking. What right have these smokers to damage our health and pollute our environment?

Finally I believe that if we all stick together, we can beat the smokers. Next week there will be an assembly telling you how to join the campaign. Shout out against smoking! Make your voice heard!

In conclusion, I would like to say that smoking is dangerous, unhealthy and wrong. Help to stop this destructive plague in our school; join our campaign today.

Yours truly,

R Harrison

Reece Harrison

Writing to Persuade

If you are writing to persuade, you want your audience to agree with you or to agree to do what you want them to, so your language needs to represent this. There are a number of language techniques which can be very effective in persuasive writing.

Techniques in Writing to Persuade

Here is a summary of some of the techniques you could use to make your writing effective as a persuasive piece:

- **Positive opening sentence** to grab the audience's attention.
- Suitable **connectives** to connect ideas and give structure to the piece.
- **Positive or negative vocabulary** to influence your reader's opinion.
- **Repetition** to emphasise your main points.
- **Direct personal address** to the reader which will make them feel more involved, e.g. use of the personal pronoun, 'you'.
- **Present tense** to make the issue seem more immediate.
- **Personal pronouns,** (e.g. I, you, he, she, they, them), give a personal tone to the issue and make the audience feel more involved.
- **Formal tone** will make your opinion seem more credible.
- **Rhetorical questions** force the reader to question the issue. These are frequently used in persuasive writing such as letters, newspaper articles and in speech writing.

- **Evidence and justification** (e.g. this had happened because…) give structure and reasoning to your opinion (use the PEE technique).
- **Comparative devices** such as similes (describing something as being like something else) and metaphors (saying something is something else) emphasise your main points.
- **Use of three:** using three words or three phrases is a good way to emphasise a point.
- **A conclusion** that links to the introduction and summarises the main points in your piece of writing.

Here is a mnemonic which might help you to remember these points: MY FOREST

M – Markers or connectives will shape your writing.
Y – You: direct (second person) address will involve the reader.

F – Facts and Formal tone, e.g. 'this had happened because…'
O – Opening statement that grabs your audience's attention.
R – Rhetorical questions and Repetition
E – Evidence and justification
S – Strong ending
T – Three (Use of)

The following is an example of a persuasive letter. Some of the persuasive techniques discussed on these pages are highlighted:

For more information on writing letters, see page 82.

Exam Practice

Write a leaflet to **persuade** the pupils at your school to take part in a 5km fun run for charity.
You could talk about…
- why pupils should take part
- the charity involved.

Opening statement grabs audience's attention

Suitable connective links the sentences

Acknowledging a different view

Suitable connective opens the paragraph

Rhetorical questions and use of three

Evidence and justification of writer's opinion

Metaphor to emphasise the point

Present tense makes the issue seem more immediate

Direct personal address through the use of a personal pronoun

Clear concluding paragraph which links to the introduction and summarises the main points

19 Clark Close
Oaklee
Bristol

Weekly News
15 High Street
Oaklee

Dear Editor,

I am writing to you to voice my opposition to the building of a supermarket on the village recreation ground. Although I am strongly against this proposal I do recognise that there are some equally important issues about the lack of a supermarket in the village that need addressing. I hope to deal with these points in my letter whilst putting forward some points that I hope you will take on board.

Firstly, if a supermarket was built it would completely destroy the recreation ground. Where would we hold our annual show? Where would the children play? Where would the cricket team play? Green space is rare in modern villages and if this were taken away our village would suffer. Also, in times of rising obesity levels, I think we need more space for our children to play, not another retail outlet selling junk food.

Secondly, our village has a very busy market and village shopping centre. If a supermarket was built the heart would be ripped out of our village; no one would shop here anymore and people would lose jobs. I appreciate that a supermarket would create some jobs but not as many as those lost.

Naturally, I agree that parking is a problem in the village and that the small village shops are expensive compared to large out-of-town supermarkets. However, have you considered how much it costs to travel to such places? Perhaps as a solution the council could put on a free bus once a week to the large supermarket.

In conclusion, I feel I have shown that the recreation ground is vital to village life in so many ways and whilst the problem of access to supermarkets does need addressing, this cannot be at the expense of village life. I look forward to hearing from you in the future.

Yours faithfully

E Burton

Mrs Eileen Burton

Writing to Advise

Writing to advise means you taking on the role of the expert, as you will be telling someone else the best, easiest or quickest way to do something.

The following points show the main things to remember when you are writing to advise:

A – Advice must be clear
D – Do keep in role
V – Vocabulary should include modal verbs
I – Informal but polite
C – Choices must be given
E – Encourage and motivate

Techniques in Writing to Advise

The suggestions below are words and phrases you may find effective to use when you are writing to advise. A selection of useful phrases is given here for each of the points shown above:

- **Advice must be clear**
  – You need to follow these three steps…
  – The first thing to do is…
  – The next step…
  – Finally…

- **Do keep in role**
  – It is my professional opinion that…
  – Many people come to me for advice…

- **Vocabulary should include modal verbs**
  (see facing page)
  – 'can', 'will', 'shall', 'may', 'could', 'would', 'should', 'might', 'must', 'ought'.

- **Informal but polite**
  – Get your friends to help you…
  – Good luck…
  – Don't panic…

- **Choices must be given**
  – You should talk to your parents or another adult…
  – Alternatively…
  – If this doesn't work then…

- **Encourage and motivate**
  – Things may seem bad but don't worry…
  – You can do this…
  – You can be successful if you…
  – I believe we can achieve anything…

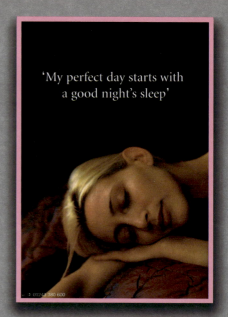

Modal Verbs

Modal verbs are a set of special verbs that are often used to help the main verb. Modal verbs cannot be used without another verb, e.g. 'I might play', 'they should come'. The modal verbs are...

can, will, must, shall, may, could, would, should, might, ought

Modals can alter the tone of your writing. The examiner will be looking for evidence of the use of modal verbs when you are giving advice.

Here is an example of writing to advise. The words and phrases given on these pages are highlighted. It is in the form of a response to a letter written to a magazine's agony aunt.

Exam Practice

Imagine you are the Head of Year 11. Write an **advice** sheet for students on how to prepare and revise for their GCSE exams. You could talk about...

- why revision and the exams are so important
- the importance of not getting stressed.

Make sure you use the tips given on these pages and try to include some modal verbs.

ask**sam**

I am a 15 year old girl studying for my GCSEs. These exams are very important to me as I want to go to university and train to be a solicitor so I'm working really hard for them.
My friends make fun of me. They say I work all the time and call me a swot and a geek. I don't want to lose my friends but I need to do well in my exams.
What should I do?
Claire, London.

Advice:
I really sympathise with you Claire: things may seem bad, but don't worry. Clearly your friends are not as sensible as you and are not taking their exams as seriously as they ought to be. Have you talked to them about how important these exams are? Many people believe that GCSE grades will determine what you do for the rest of your life. You could try explaining to your friends how important it is for you to do well. Tell them your ambitions for the future and that you'd like them to support you. Alternatively, try getting them to help you – you could set up a revision club. If these ideas don't work then it might be that the people you call your friends are not really true friends. I think you should concentrate on your own future – you might not even know your friends in two years' time. You can be successful and get into your dream job if you work hard enough for your exams. Good luck!

Encouraging phrases which offer sympathy	Informal and friendly tone
Suitable connective	Giving choices
Modal verb	Keeping role as an expert
Introducing evidence	Phrase to encourage and motivate

Exam Tips

Useful Words and Phrases for the Exam

There are certain words and phrases that can be very useful in writing to argue, persuade or advise. Some of these words and phrases are given here with descriptions of how and when you should use them.

- **To state your opinions:** these phrases indicate that what follows is your personal opinion. They are polite and quite formal, and are therefore useful in letters and speeches etc.
  - I feel / think / consider…
  - In my opinion…
  - I am convinced that…

- **To link your ideas / opinions:** these connectives (see page 34) make your writing flow well.
  - Firstly…
  - Secondly…
  - In addition…
  - A further consideration must be…
  - Similarly…

- **To introduce evidence:** these phrases can be useful in backing up your idea or opinion.
  - It has come to my attention that…
  - A recent survey in the school newspaper found that…

- **To give the alternative view:** these phrases help to justify your opinion, by implying that other people have the same opinion as you.
  - Some people have said that…
  - Some people believe that…
  - Many people think…

- **To present a balanced view:** these connectives suggest that a new idea / opinion will follow. They are used when one idea / opinion has been discussed, and a new one is being introduced.
  - However…
  - On the other hand…
  - Nevertheless…

- **To be convincing (but polite):** these phrases show that you accept that other opinions can be valid.
  - Clearly some people will have opposing views, but I believe…
  - I understand your objections…
  - I am sure you will agree that…

- **To discredit the other opinion:** these phrases suggest that there is evidence to prove that the other opinion / idea is wrong and that an explanation will follow to say why it is wrong.
  - Clearly, this is not true…
  - However, this is not the case…
  - This is misleading…

Checking your Work

You should spend five minutes of your time in the exam checking your answer. It is easy to make mistakes with spelling, punctuation and grammar when you are under pressure so it is important to read through your answer carefully when you have finished it.

Make sure you have…
- used paragraphs
- linked your paragraphs with suitable connectives (see page 34)
- used a variety of punctuation correctly
- spelt most words correctly
- crossed out any mistakes neatly and written your corrections so that the examiner can clearly understand your intentions.

Paper 2

Section A:

Section B:

Reading Poetry from Different Cultures

The Exam Question

Section A of Paper 2 will test your knowledge and understanding of poetry from different cultures. You will have already read the poems and made notes in your anthology to help you to revise. Remember that in the exam you will have a clean copy of the anthology so you won't have your notes to help you. Make sure you read each poem at least six times before the exam. You will have a choice of two questions which will ask you to compare two or more poems in terms of culture and traditions. You should spend about 45 minutes answering **one** of these questions.

What is the examiner looking for?

The examiner wants to see that you can read, understand and compare poetry. You must show that you can do the following:

- Comment on the content, themes, setting and style of a poem.
- Comment on stylistic features, such as those on pages 6-7, and the effects that they produce.
- Comment on any presentational devices that are used (e.g. font sizes, the layout of the words on the page, the length, order and structure of the verses).
- Compare the poems and refer to the other poems.
- Select relevant material and quotes from the poems. Remember that short quotes are best; do not write out whole verses.
- Write about how language changes and varies according to the characters that are using the language, or the time the poem was written.

The PEE Technique

Always use the 'PEE' technique in your answers. This reminds you that you must have a three part response to your answers:

P   Make a **P**oint
E   Use **E**vidence from the poem (a quote)
E   Give an **E**xplanation to back up the point you are making. Explain why the evidence illustrates your point.

For example:

P   The salwar kameez that is sent to the girl in the poem *Presents from My Aunts in Pakistan* is beautiful.
E   It is described as 'glistening like an orange split open'.
E   This simile portrays its shining beauty and yet, whilst the girl can appreciate its splendour, she would rather wear a pair of jeans. She feels that she cannot be as beautiful as the clothes that she is sent.

Culture and Traditions

What are Culture and Traditions?

You should be familiar with the terms **culture** and **traditions**.

Culture is a person's background with reference to their language, their way of life and their beliefs. Traditions are associated with different cultures. They are customs that people of a particular culture uphold. For example, typical traditions of the British culture would include having a Sunday lunch or celebrating Bonfire Night.

All the poems that you have studied in the anthology cover aspects of different cultures and traditions. You must be able to recognise features of different cultures and traditions and be able to write about them in the exam.

Culture

Culture refers to...
- people's origins and backgrounds (where they are originally from)
- the language that people speak
- traditions that people uphold
- the way that people are expected to behave in a particular society
- the politics of a particular country or society
- people's beliefs (religion).

Traditions

Traditions refer to...
- the way that people behave in certain situations
- things that people say
- events, festivals and celebrations associated with a particular culture.

You need to have a clear idea of what these terms actually mean to enable you to write about them effectively in the exam.

Poetry Terms

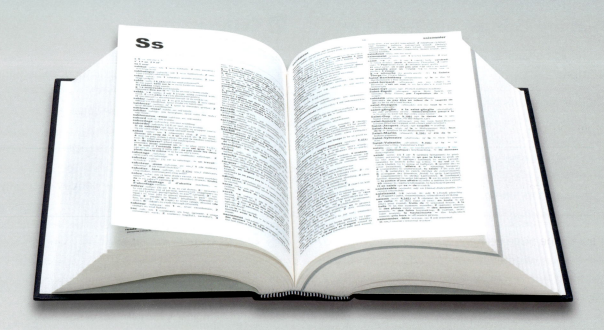

For all the poems that you have studied you should be able to explain each in terms of…

- **content:** what the poem is about
- **setting:** where / when the poem is set, for example a country, a village, a house, or a time in history
- **themes:** issues the writer wants to highlight and / or wants the reader to think about
- **style:** the way that the writer uses words (diction) in their poems; the words that they choose, and the effect that they have on the reader.

You should use the correct terms to help you describe how language is used in a poem. Here is a reminder of the main terms (see also pages 6-7):

- **Accent:** the way a character would sound if he / she spoke aloud
- **Adjectives:** describe nouns
- **Adverbs:** describe the action
- **Alliteration:** repetition of a sound at the beginning of words
- **Assonance:** rhyme of the internal vowel sound
- **Contrast:** a strong difference between two things
- **Dialect:** words and grammar used by different groups
- **Exclamations:** portray emotions
- **Imagery:** words so descriptive they create a picture in the reader's mind
- **Irony and sarcasm:** the use of words to imply the opposite of their meaning
- **Juxtaposition:** the positioning of words / phrases / ideas close together for effect

- **Metaphor:** an image created by referring to something as something else
- **Onomatopoeia:** words that sound like their meaning
- **Personification:** giving an object human qualities
- **Puns / play on words:** words used in an amusing way to suggest other meanings
- **Questions (interrogatives)**
- **Received Pronunciation:** a prestigious accent (used by many newsreaders)
- **Repetition:** words, phrases, sentences or structures which are repeated
- **Rhetorical questions:** questions that don't require answers; the answer is obvious
- **Rhyme:** the use of rhyming words to affect the sound pattern
- **Rhythm:** the beat of the poem when read aloud
- **Simile:** a comparison that includes the word 'as' or 'like'
- **Standard English:** the standard use of words and grammar
- **Symbolism:** symbols that represents an abstract idea
- **Tone:** the overall attitude of the poem.

Helpful Hint

You may come across the terms stanza, diction and persona. Stanza is another word for verse. Diction is another word for vocabulary (words). Persona refers to a character in a poem.

Limbo Edward Kamau Brathwaite

Limbo can mean three things so the poem exists on three levels:
- Limbo the dance
- Limbo the place between heaven and hell
- In limbo - stuck in the middle of two situations.

Content

The poem is about slaves being brought from Africa to America, and the hardships they suffered. It describes the African limbo dance being performed. In a limbo dance a stick is lowered so the dancer must keep getting closer to the ground to get under it. In terms of slavery, the people were beaten to the ground and subjugated (forcibly disciplined) to the will of their owners. The slaves were then in limbo of the third kind - trapped between their backgrounds and free selves, and their new lives as slaves.

Setting

Africa is evoked through phrases such as 'sun coming up' and 'the dumb gods'. Limbo is an ancient dance native to the African people which reminds us of their traditional culture and lifestyle.

The deck of a slave ship is referred to as 'the dark deck', which also evokes an image of Hell.

Themes

These are echoed through the title of the poem.
- People being in limbo (trapped in two different situations), like the African slaves.
- The way that ancient traditions survive time, like the limbo dance.
- Slavery and corruption, and the subjugation of human beings to the will of others.
- The strength of the spirit and free will, enabling people to survive in ill-fated circumstances.
- The clash of cultures; the slaves and their masters had different languages which led to a 'silence' between them.

Style

- Strong **rhythm** and **rhyme** echoes the limbo music.
- **Symbolism:** the stick is a symbol of oppression. The character gets lower to the ground and closer to being a total slave. At times in the poem the stick is a whip with which the slaves are beaten.
- **Imagery:** the image of rape is evident: 'knees spread wide' and the physical force into the ground represents the domination of the slave owners over the slaves. Images of darkness, oppression and violence pervade the poem at the beginning.
- **Repetition** of 'limbo like me' makes the reader consider the phrase and the wide variety of its meanings, and suggests the suffering is ongoing.
- **Negative diction**, e.g. 'dark', 'silence', stresses the loneliness of being in captivity and the despair the people felt.
- By line 40 more **positive images** enter the poem: the sun symbolises a bright new life, and 'raising me' and 'saving me' suggest a period of hope.

Nothing's Changed Tatamkhulu Afrika

Content

The poem is about a man's journey to a district that has changed in recent years. The area is District Six which was an area only for white people during apartheid. Now anybody can go there. It is being redeveloped and now houses smart restaurants. However, at the time the poem was written many black people in South Africa would not have been able to afford to go there, or were not made to feel welcome. This makes the poet angry. It is as if apartheid still exists in the country, even though legally it was abolished in 1990.

Setting

The poem is set in District Six, an area in Cape Town, South Africa that was declared for whites only during 1964, leading to the eviction of thousands of black and mixed-race citizens. This was during apartheid (a law that separated black and white people).

The area is one of contrast: the upper class restaurant with linen table cloths and single roses on the tables, and the working man's café down the road which sells local food and has plastic tables and spit on the floor. The character looks in through the window of the smart restaurant. The setting represents the differences in the living standards of some black and white communities in South Africa, even today.

Themes

- Apartheid: racial separation, leading to one being considered inferior (not as good).
- Racial discrimination.
- Anger and frustration caused by unfairness in society.
- Alienation: feeling excluded (left out) from society, '…we know where we belong.'
- The impact of childhood memories; they remain with us throughout our lives.

Style

- **Contrast** between the luxurious setting of the smart restaurant and the cheap café.
- **Symbolism:** District Six (the most famous community from which black and mixed-race citizens were evicted) represents apartheid. The glass in the window represents the racial divide.
- **Assonance**, e.g. 'ice white' and 'spit a little', is used to stress the character's anger.
- **Alliteration** of the harsh 'c' sound, e.g. 'into trouser cuffs, cans', expresses the poet's anger.
- **Angry diction** expresses how the poet is feeling, e.g. 'anger of my eyes', 'mean mouth', 'a bomb, to shiver down the glass'.
- **Onomatopoeia**, e.g. 'click', 'crunch,' 'spit'. These words help us to follow the man on his journey through the district, literally and **metaphorically**.

Island Man Grace Nichols

Content

The poem is about a man who once lived on an island in the Caribbean but now lives in London. He still wakes up every morning to sounds and happy memories of the Caribbean. The Caribbean morning that he thinks he has woken to contrasts sharply with the reality of his life in London.

Setting

The poem is set in London, but the place that is described beautifully is the island in the Caribbean. London is described as 'grey' and 'dull'.

Themes

- Feeling separated from home: the man misses his home on the Caribbean island.
- Alienation and loneliness.
- Love of your homeland (where you come from): we can tell that the man thinks favourably about his homeland through the words that are used to describe it.
- Imagination (what goes on in your mind) and reality.
- The impact of childhood: the man's memories of the island on which he grew up.

Style

- **Imagery:** the words used help us to picture the Caribbean island. We can almost see waves crashing on the beach and the fishermen preparing for their fishing trip.
- **Appealing to the senses** (sight, sound, touch): we can 'hear' the waves crashing on the beach, and the sound of the gulls.
- **Contrast** of the beautiful Caribbean island ('emerald island') with the busy London road ('North Circular roar'). The 'blue surf' contrasts with the 'grey metallic soar' of London.

- **Different levels of meaning:** 'wombing' (a reference to the womb, where a baby develops) indicates the richness of the sea and the life it contains and stresses the fact that the man was born in the Caribbean.
- **Repetition** and **alliteration**, e.g. 'groggily, groggily' stress the man's feelings in the poem and give them importance. He is disappointed when he remembers he is in London.
- **Effective use of verbs**, e.g. 'heaves' shows that the man is reluctant to face the reality of his day in London.
- **Alliteration:** the 'sound of the blue surf', appeals to our senses by echoing the sound of the sea.
- The **absence of punctuation** allows the poem to flow, giving it a dream-like quality.

Blessing Imtiaz Dharker

Content

The poem describes the scene in an Indian village when a water pipe bursts. The children play in the stream of water whilst the adults collect water in any containers they can find. The poem portrays what a precious commodity water is in villages like this.

Setting

The poem is set in an Indian village that has been without water for some time. The 'skin' (soil) of the village 'cracks like a pod' when the water pipe bursts. The scene is described vividly; the people rush around the village, and the children play in the 'liquid sun'.

Themes

- The simplicity of life in many villages around the world: the people in the poem have basic needs; they value water ('the blessing'), something that other societies take for granted.
- The power of nature: water can transform a scene and the lives of the people in it.
- The daily struggle to survive in developing countries: the children are having fun but the poem refers to their 'small bones', reminding us that they are weak and undernourished. We are also told at the beginning of the poem, 'there never is enough water'.

Style

- **Positive diction**, e.g. 'kindly', 'silver', 'sun', 'polished to perfection', 'the sudden rush of fortune'. These positive words emphasise what a blessing the water is.
- **Appealing to the senses:** we can picture the scene through the images in the poem and we can 'hear' the effects of the water through the use of **onomatopoeia**, e.g. 'splash', 'rush', 'crashes'.
- Short lines and phrases echo the sounds of the rain falling and the drops of water.
- **Similes**, e.g. 'the skin cracks like a pod'; this describes how dry the land is. The image created makes the scene more vivid for the reader.
- **Metaphors:** the sound of the water is so good that it sounds like 'the voice of a kindly god'.
- **Personification** is used in this metaphor. The water is given human (in fact superhuman) qualities and appreciated as something special.
- Religious **imagery**, e.g. the phrase 'a roar of tongues' reminds us of a choir singing. The people are referred to as a 'congregation' which is what we call a group of people in church, and the title of the poem 'Blessing' is a part of a church service.

Many thanks to Oxfam for use of image from:
www.oxfam.org.uk/atwork/emerg/wateremg.html
© Oxfam GB. Reproduced by permission

Two Scavengers in a Truck... Lawrence Ferlinghetti

Content

The poem describes two garbage men in their garbage truck waiting at some traffic lights alongside a glamorous young couple in a Mercedes. The two vehicles and their occupants could not be more different. On a deeper level the poem is about injustice (unfairness) in some societies. The poem questions whether America is really a democracy.

Setting

The poem is set in San Francisco, America, at some traffic lights on a main street.

Themes

- Social injustice: in some societies there seem to be two social groups; the couple in the car and the garbage men represent these groups. The easy lifestyle of the wealthy (the architect in his Mercedes) contrasts with the hard life of the garbage men who have been clinging to the back of the garbage truck since 4am.
- America is often referred to as the 'land of dreams' where people can be whatever they want to be, but here the poet suggests that this is not true. The garbage men watch the couple as if watching a television advert where people can do whatever they want. The poet mentions a television advert to reinforce that the idea that people are free to do what they want and be who they want to be is not a reality.
- Political protest: although both sets of people work, their jobs and lifestyles are very different.

Style

- The poem has a **narrative** quality; it reads like a story. The language is simple and direct, and the lack of punctuation allows the scene to unfold without interruption.
- **Contrast** is used effectively throughout the poem to stress the differences between the characters. Contrast starts in the poem's title with 'scavengers' (creatures that pick up others people's leftovers) and 'beautiful', 'truck' and 'Mercedes'. The two couples are **juxtaposed** throughout the poem to highlight the contrast between them.
- **Repetition:** certain phrases are repeated in slightly different forms, e.g. lines 30 and 33. This emphasises that the poet does not believe this is true and wants the reader to consider this idea carefully.
- **Alliteration** is used to stress key points about the characters, e.g. the use of 'c' in line 28.
- **Adjectives** are used to paint the scene vividly in the reader's mind.
- **Similes:** the garbage man is described as a 'gargoyle' and 'Quasimodo'; an ugly creature. A gargoyle is one of the stone faces found on the sides of churches, and Quasimodo is the hunchback from the story *The Hunchback of Notre Dame*.
- The **layout** (the way that the poem looks on the page) is unusual and therefore highlights the unusual social situation that the poet is describing.

Helpful Hint

You can use shortened versions of the poems' titles in the exam (e.g. 'Two Scavengers'), as long as you write enough of the title for the examiner to know which poem you are referring to.

Night of the Scorpion Nissim Ezekiel

Content

The poet describes a night in his village when he was a little boy and his mother was stung by a scorpion. All the villagers came to help and tried to make his mother better. His father was worried, and although he was normally a very rational man, he tried all sorts of strange remedies (cures), such as putting paraffin on the sting and lighting it. The holy man also performed some rituals to try to cure her. His mother recovers and is just glad that the scorpion stung her and not one of her children.

Setting

The poem is set in a village in India. Everywhere is very wet following heavy rain. The primitive (basic) village is described in detail by the poet's references to the neighbours and their behaviour, their mud-baked huts and the holy man who is called upon to help.

Themes

- The selfless love that mothers have for their children. The character's (poet's) mother is glad that she was stung rather than one of her children.
- The closeness of some communities; everyone came out to help showing real community spirit (a society where people look after each other).
- The strength of childhood memories: the poet remembers the night in great detail.

Style

- The poem has a **narrative** quality; it is in free verse and reads like a story.
- **Imagery:** the idea that the scorpion is the devil runs throughout the poem. The words 'evil' and 'diabolic' are used in reference to it.
- **Rhythm:** the rhythms of the lines echo normal speech so we feel that we are listening to a story being told.
- **Similes:** the peasants are compared to flies, suggesting that there are many of them dashing around making lots of noise.
- **Repetition** of 'may'. Chants are used by the peasants, suggesting that they are superstitious and believe that such actions can cure the woman. The holy man is sent for, not a doctor as we would expect in our society.
- **Negative diction** is used to describe the mother's pain, e.g. in lines 34 and 35.

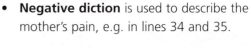

Vultures Chinua Achebe

Content

The poem describes two vultures in a tree. The day before, they ate the insides of a dead animal, however today they are being affectionate towards one another.

The poem highlights how love and brutality can exist side by side. It also makes this point by describing a commandant in a German concentration camp: during the day he is involved in the burning of the Jews, but on the way home he stops to buy chocolate for his children.

The poet is stating that there can be goodness in the most evil heart. But he makes the point at the end of the poem that even in love there can be an element of evil.

Setting

The poem is set in the plains of Nigeria and the concentration camps of Nazi Germany.

Themes

- The duality of life (the two sides to everything).
- The many sides to the human heart.
- The contrast between nature and human nature: the vultures have to eat the dead animal to survive; the camp commandant kills people because he has been ordered to.

Style

- The lines are irregular in length and there is **no regular rhyme** scheme. This helps to reinforce the idea that nature and human beings are unpredictable.
- **Irony:** it is ironic that the commandant is part of the cruel process of gassing the Jewish people, but he has the kindness to stop and buy chocolate for his children.
- **Contrast:** the poem opens with **bleak diction**, e.g. 'greyness' and 'drizzle', yet the vultures lean towards each other 'affectionately'. The commandant goes home with the smell of 'human roast clinging' to his nostrils, but he is going home to his 'tender offspring'. This contrast stresses the theme of duality (two sides to things). The poem alternates between **positive and negative diction**. (It is worth underlining them in your poem if you have not already done so.)
- **Alliteration:** e.g. 'drizzle of one despondent dawn'. This sentence sets the scene for the poem.
- **Metaphors**, e.g. 'a pebble on a stem…'. This metaphor stresses the ugliness of the vultures, and 'icy caverns of a cruel heart' uses **negative diction** to emphasise the point.

What Were They Like? Denise Levertov

Content

The poem is a series of questions and answers about the Vietnamese war which lasted from 1954 until 1975. The Americans became involved in the war and there were many killings on both sides. Many people thought America should not have joined in the war, as it was a civil war (a war between the people of that country).

The second stanza starts with the word 'Sir' which suggests that a soldier is being questioned. The poem describes what the Vietnamese people were like before the war; how they lived happily and worked in the rice fields, but then the war changed everything.

Setting

We don't know where the poem is set – it is written as a conversation between two people. The soldier (poet) is describing Vietnam in South East Asia before and after the war.

It is suggested that before the war Vietnam was a beautiful and tranquil place with lanterns lighting the paths, and pretty blossoms. After the war the place was filled with charred bones, dead children, and bombed and silent fields.

Themes

- The atrocities of war: how people's lives can be destroyed by war.
- Celebration of another culture: the way that the poet writes about Vietnam and its people before the war suggests that the place was beautiful and the people were happy.

Style

- The poem is laid out as a set of **questions** in the first stanza, which are answered in the second.
- In the first stanza the language is conversational in tone and direct in style.
- The second stanza is full of **poetic phrases** as it describes the place before the war with its people whose 'speech…was like a song'. The **alliteration** stresses the positive qualities of the Vietnamese.
- **Alliteration** with the soft 'm' sound, 'moths in moonlight', emphasises the peace and quiet of the country before the war.
- **Interrogatives** are used to make the reader consider particular subjects. The soldier is being asked the questions, but so too are the readers of the poem. The title itself is a question.
- **Violent words** and **images** are used throughout the poem to show the poet's disapproval of the war – 'hearts turned to stone,' 'bitter to the burned mouth' (describes people who had their mouths burned by the napalm bombs), 'bombs smashed those mirrors' and 'time only to scream'.
- **Positive diction** is applied to the place and people before the war, e.g. 'pleasant ways,' and 'delight in blossom'. The speech of the Vietnamese is described as being 'like a song'.
- **Contrast** is used effectively in the poem to stress what the country was like before and after the war. This enables the tone of the poem to convey the poet's disapproval of the war.

(From) Search for My Tongue Sujata Bhatt

Content

The woman in the poem is expressing how difficult it is to be bilingual (able to speak two languages) because you are never sure which language to use. She is making the point that it is difficult to be part of two cultures as you are unsure whether you actually belong to either culture. She has a dream where her mother tongue (the language she grew up speaking) grows in her mouth like a flower. This part of the poem is written in Gujarati, which is her mother tongue. The dream reminds the woman that she still has her mother tongue.

Setting

The poem does not have an obvious setting; it is in the thoughts of the woman. Her mouth becomes the setting, in her dream, as it turns into a growing garden.

Themes

- Cultural identity: belonging to two different cultures (in this case Indian and American) and the problems this brings.
- Belonging: the need for people to fit in with certain groups to give them a sense of belonging.

Style

- An **image** of the woman's mother tongue as a growing, living thing runs throughout the poem. It is given a **positive significance** - as it is referred to as blossom (fresh and pretty flowers).
- The title of the poem means two things: the search for the woman's mother tongue and the search for her cultural identity.
- The section that deals with the difficulty of speaking two languages has **harsh diction**, e.g. 'rot', 'die' and 'spit'. The **repetition** of these words also emphasises the frustration and anger she feels.
- **Assonance**, e.g. on lines 13 ('mouth') and 14 ('out') stresses the **negative diction.**
- The **Gujarati** stands out in the poem. It could show that she feels she stands out because she speaks this language. It describes the language flowering in her mouth as she is asleep, and is full of **positive diction**.
- **Metaphors:** the idea of the woman's mother tongue as a bud (a natural, growing thing) runs throughout the poem.

(From) Unrelated Incidents Tom Leonard

Content

The poem is about attitudes towards non-standard accents and dialects. It is written as a phonetic (written as it sounds) transcript of a Glaswegian accent. The character in the poem is pretending to be a newsreader to make the point that just because he does not use Standard English (as newsreaders do) it does not mean that he isn't trustworthy. He is commenting on the snobbery associated with accents. People presume things about people because of their accents.

Setting

The poet uses a Glaswegian accent, suggesting that he comes from Glasgow. However, there is no actual setting to this poem as it is written like a speech, rather than a story.

Themes

- Standard English and Received Pronunciation are regarded as the dialect and accent of status and authority.
- Social identity (like the cultural identity that we see in other poems): the man belongs to a particular social group and he uses the language of that group. However, he is aware that some people might look down on him because of the way he speaks.

- Injustice in society: in this poem the poet states that people are judged by the language they use. He says that people might think he is a 'scruff' because of his accent.
- The truth: the poem challenges what we mean by the truth. The truth can be different things to different people. He thinks that all accents are equal; this is his truth, but others would not agree with him.

Style

- **Dialectal words and phrases** are used throughout the poem, e.g. 'belt up', 'coz', and 'scruff'. They are used to show to which social group the persona (character) in the poem belongs. He values the way that he speaks and feels that it is good enough to use in his poem.
- The poem starts with language that is close to **Standard English** but it becomes more **dialectal** as it progresses.
- The poet ends the poem with the rather **aggressive phrase** 'belt up', expressing his anger with people who look down on non-standard accents and suggesting that these people should shut up.
- The **layout** is very unusual as it uses very short lines. It looks like a television autocue which newsreaders read from. This highlights the contrast between the accent and dialect used by newsreaders, and the strong Scottish accent and non-standard dialect used by the character in the poem.

Half-Caste John Agard

Content

The poem is an objection to the term 'half-caste' used to mean 'of mixed race'. It is written in the form of a monologue. The poet objects to the use of the word 'half' because half of something is not as good as a full item, and so the term 'half-caste' implies that people of mixed race are inferior. Although the poem treats the topic with some humour, the underlying anger at the situation is never very far from the surface.

Setting

The poem is set as though the poet is speaking to people who use the term 'half-caste'. It is an English language term which means the poet is referring to English-speaking societies. The poem's setting is society in general but it does refer to 'england weather', suggesting that the poet may be referring more specifically to English society.

Themes

- The problem of applying a term to a group of people as it can cause offence.
- Racial prejudice: some people have different views of people who have different coloured skin to their own and treat them differently.

Style

- The introduction to the poem is like a greeting and 'excuse me' is used **sarcastically** by the character to apologise for being different.
- The poem is a dramatic **monologue** (a piece that could be performed on stage). Monologues are often used to make comments about society as they are quite direct in tone and use the second person ('you'). Punctuation often isn't used because it is supposed to sound like speech.
- The poem is written in the **first person** ('I', 'me') so the reader feels involved in the character's thoughts and feelings.
- It is written in a Caribbean **dialect**, which is a form of **creole** (a language or dialect based on two or more languages). This shows that the poet values this form of language, but he also uses it to mock the attitudes of people who consider him to be 'half-caste'.
- The poem presents the reader with a series of funny **images**, e.g. 'standing on one leg', 'close

half-a-eye'. This **humorous** tone shows that the poet does not take the people who term him half-caste seriously. He tells them to open their minds and use their whole brain to see him for what he is – a human being.

- The poet wishes people could see 'wid de whole of yu eye'. This **metaphoric phrase** means he wishes people could see things as they really are.
- **Repetition** of the word 'half', and the many different contexts the poet puts it into, emphasise the stupidity of using the term 'half-caste'.

Love After Love Derek Walcott

Content

The poem is about self-discovery – learning, accepting and celebrating who you are, and valuing all the things that have made you what you are.

The poem describes how we often ignore our own needs in order to give attention to other people, but we should make time for ourselves and value our own lives. The poet values his past and all the experiences that have made him who he is today, even the painful experiences.

Setting

The poem is set in a metaphorical house (not a real one, one in your mind). It is set in our own past, present and future. It is a theoretical setting.

Themes

- The value of the past in helping us to grow up: the importance of our backgrounds and the things that we have experienced in the past.
- The importance of being comfortable and happy with who we are.

Style

- There is a series of **metaphors** in the poem. For example, the mirror is the way that we see ourselves and look back at the past, the sentence 'feast on your life' makes life seem like a delicious banquet which should be enjoyed to the full, and the person that is greeted at the door is our old self (how we used to be).
- **Religious diction** is used, e.g. 'Give wine. Give bread'. These words are part of religious services and give a formal, but sincere and caring, tone to the poem.
- The ideas in the poem are complex, but the language used is very simple.
- The poem reads like a series of instructions on how to accept yourself for what you are, and rejoice in what you find.

Helpful Hint

Don't forget that the examiner wants to see your thoughts and opinions too, not just those that you have read in the revision guide.

This Room Imtiaz Dharker

Content

Like other poems (e.g. *Limbo* and *Two Scavengers*), the poem exists on more than one level.

The poem describes a room that has gone wild; all the items in it are trying to escape. They are in search of 'space, light and empty air' (freedom).

On another level, the room is the metaphor used to describe the person in the poem, who feels that it is time to break away from the predictable. The character is given the chance to do this 'when the improbable arrives' (when something unexpected happens). The poet is saying that we should welcome times like this and use them as a chance to escape from the way that things have been in the past. The poem celebrates the fact that life is exciting. The reader can feel the excitement through the images that are used and the way that the poem is written.

Setting

The poem's setting is a house, from which the rooms and their contents are trying to escape.

Themes

- Celebration of the fact that life can be unpredictable.
- Celebration of personal growth and the lives that we have.
- The fact that change can be a good, exciting thing, rather than something to worry about.
- Freedom: freedom is the most important element in our lives and we should make the most of it.

Style

- The poem is written in **free verse** (no structure to the verses) which helps to put across the message that nothing is more valuable than our freedom.
- **Personification:** the room is portrayed as a person who is full of energy.
- **Imagery:** the pots, pans and the bed are images used to represent the quest for freedom.
- **Present participle:** the verbs are in the -ing form (e.g. 'breaking', 'clapping', 'lifting'). This adds immediacy to the poem and makes it sound as if it is happening now, which enables the reader to get involved in the action.
- **Alliteration,** e.g. 'corners...crash through the clouds'. These harsh sounds are in keeping with the idea of breaking out and escaping.

- **Onomatopoeia** is used to enhance the sound effects of the poem. You can 'hear' some of the words, e.g. 'cracking', 'crash', and 'clang'.
- The poem **appeals to the senses** (sight and sound) to emphasise the pleasure of being alive and free.
- The poem is full of movement, which is reinforced by the use of **enjambment** (where one line runs into the next without a break).

Not My Business Niyi Osundare

Content

The poem is about unfair treatment of citizens by the authorities. It explains what could happen if people ignore the bad treatment of others.

The first character in the poem is beaten up and taken away in a jeep. The second character is taken away and imprisoned. The third character loses her job for no reason, even though she was a good worker. The poet describes how those who are not directly affected do not seem to care as long as they themselves are safe and have enough to eat ('the yam'). However, in the final stanza the persona (who ignored the unfair treatment of the others) becomes the target of the injustice when the jeep that is used to take people away arrives at his house.

The poet is trying to convey the message that we cannot ignore injustice just because it does not affect us. It is short-sighted because eventually injustice affects everybody.

Setting

The poem is set in Nigeria, Africa: the names of the characters are Nigerian and the poet was born in Nigeria.

Themes

- Injustice and inequality in society.
- Self-preservation: people often turn a blind eye as long as they themselves are alright. However this situation can have disastrous consequences, as shown in the poem when eventually the injustice affects the character who turned a blind eye and 'they' come to collect him.
- Persecution of citizens by the authorities.

Style

- **Violent diction** is used throughout the poem, e.g. 'beat', 'stuffed him', 'dragged', and 'booted'. This vividly describes what happens in each case so that the reader can share the horror of the situation.
- **Repetition** is used throughout the poem to stress the issues, e.g. 'no query, no warning, no probe' and 'what business of mine…so long they don't take the yam'. Repetition of 'they' shows that the arrival of 'them' is a regular occurrence.
- **Similes,** e.g. 'soft like clay'. This simile describes how badly the man was beaten. He became as soft as clay.
- The last line of the poem describes the threat. The **alliteration** makes the line sound quiet and ominous, just like the jeep waiting on the lawn.
- **Metaphor:** 'froze my hungry hand'. This emphasises the terror the character feels by the fact that he can't eat, despite being very hungry.
- **Interrogatives:** 'What business … savouring mouth?' This question is repeated throughout the poem after every injustice, as though the character wants to justify his ignorance. He tries to get the reader to relate to his situation.
- The fact that the poem mentions 'one morning', 'one night', 'one day' and 'one evening', emphasises that injustice can occur at any time.

Presents from My Aunts... Moniza Alvi

Content

The poem is about a young girl who was born in Pakistan but lives in England and so she belongs to two cultures.

The girl's aunts send her traditional clothes from Pakistan, but she says she would rather be dressed in western fashions. She feels that the Pakistani clothes are too beautiful for her to wear. She mentions all the things that her aunts have sent: a salwar kameez (traditional trousers and tunic) and slippers, a camel skin lamp for her parents' bedroom, and some beautiful Indian jewellery for her mother (which was later stolen).

She remembers that she came from Pakistan by boat and stayed at her grandmother's house. She tries to remember her homeland by looking at old photos, and comments on how Pakistan has been 'fractured' by a territorial war (a war over land). Finally, she imagines herself back in Pakistan, looking through the gates of some gardens. She is on the outside looking in. This reflects how she feels about living in England – that she is not fully integrated, that she belongs to two different cultures, and this sometimes causes her conflict.

Setting

The poem is set in England where the girl lives. Images of Pakistan are given through her memories and the things she remembers from the old photos. In the last stanza, the girl imagines she is at the Shalimar ornamental gardens in Lahore, a city in Pakistan.

Themes

- The problems and frustration caused by belonging to two cultures.
- Fond memories of the past and childhood.
- How our cultural backgrounds shape who we become.
- Alienation – feeling left out.

Style

- The poem is long and detailed (a **narrative**) to enable us to share her story and her emotions.
- The first stanza describes strong, rich colours (e.g. 'orange', 'gold', 'candy-striped', 'apple-green', and 'silver') to represent the Asian culture.

- **Imagery** is used throughout the poem to enable us to visualise (see) scenes and items, e.g. the salwar kameez is described as, 'glistening like an orange split open'. The lamp in line 27 is described with colours 'like stained glass'.
- The poet mentions the 'fractured land / throbbing through newsprint'. Here she is referring to the conflict over Kashmir (an area belonging to both Pakistan and India). In amongst her personal reflections is a political comment.
- The conflict between her cultures is shown by the way she writes about each one in detail.
- **Metaphors,** e.g. 'I was aflame', 'throbbing through newsprint' highlight the character's feelings.
- The two cultures are **juxtaposed** throughout the poem to reinforce the contrast between them.
- **Positive and negative diction** is juxtaposed throughout to contrast the two cultures and to show the problems that arise when the two cultures meet.

Hurricane Hits England Grace Nichols

Content

The poem describes a hurricane, which makes the woman in the poem remember the hurricanes that used to strike in her homeland of Guyana in the Caribbean.

The hurricane is frightening, but it is also welcomed as it reminds her of her life in Guyana before she came to England, and she has fond memories of that past. The hurricane represents her inner turmoil at belonging to two cultures. She refers to ancient gods and uses language from her Caribbean culture to show this turmoil (like other poems in the anthology). The storm awakens experiences and memories from her past.

At the end of the poem the character realises that, despite all the turmoil inside and all around her, all that matters is being alive and having a place on this earth. This is the 'sweet mystery' of life.

Setting

The poem is set in England where the woman now lives. However, it also refers to Guyana in the past.

Themes

- The force of nature.
- The strength of memories from the past and the effect they can have on your life.
- The importance of culture and language.
- The inner turmoil that people belonging to two different cultures might experience; the outside storm reflects her inner battles.

Style

- **Negative diction,** e.g. 'howling', 'rage', 'dark' and 'fearful'. These words describe the storm and the experience of living in a new land.
- Traditional Caribbean gods are called upon – 'Huracan', 'Oya' and 'Shango' (gods of winds and storms). The woman's thoughts go back to her original place of birth and this is shown by using language from this culture.
- **Religious chants** are evoked in the last two stanzas: 'I am…', 'Come to…'. This shows the woman's respect for the storm (the power of nature) and the feelings that it creates in her.
- **Interrogatives:** there are many questions in the poem which show that the woman is questioning herself and her feelings, for example, 'O why is my heart unchained?'. Here she is asking herself why she feels the way that she does (that is, tossed and uprooted by the storm).
- **Juxtaposition** of 'fearful' and 'reassuring' emphasises the woman's mixed feelings.
- The poem uses the **third person** ('she') in the first stanza, which shows that she doesn't feel comfortable with herself and how she fits in. It then changes to **first person** ('I', 'me') which shows the woman is no longer scared – she is thinking of her homeland – she feels she fits in, in her homeland, and can be herself.

Comparing Poems

In the exam you will be asked to compare poems; this means writing about aspects that are similar in two or more poems. This may be the themes, setting, language (style) features, or layout. For example,

- Racial prejudice (theme) is discussed in *Nothing's Changed* and *Half-Caste*.
- Both *Blessing* and *Night of the Scorpion* are set in small, close-knit Indian villages (setting).
- The use of dialectal words and phrases (style) appear in both *Unrelated Incidents* and *Half-Caste*.
- *Blessing* and *This Room* look similar on the page (layout), set out in free verse (no consistent structure to the verses).

The following example question will give you an idea of what you may be asked to do.

Q. Write about the ways in which two poems describe incidents or events. Make sure you…
- say what incident or event is described
- discuss and compare the language used to describe the incident or event in each poem.

You need to be aware of the poems' similarities (and differences) in order to answer the exam questions. The question above asks you for…
- descriptions of the incidents or events in two poems. Events occur in many of the poems so you have a good choice.
- explanations and evidence of how language is used in the poems you have chosen to describe the incidents or events.
- similarities and differences between the language used in the poems you have chosen.

To answer this question successfully you need to think of two poems in which an incident or event takes place and then describe how language is used in each of the poems to portray the events.

Your answer should include a short introduction which is relevant to the question. You should also say in your introduction which poems you will be comparing. You should then go on to compare the two poems you named in your introduction. You could conclude your answer by giving your overall opinion e.g. on whether the poems use language in similar ways, or in very different ways. You could even say which poem you think uses language in the most effective way.

The questions are designed so that you can show that you can write about the poems' content, setting, themes and style.

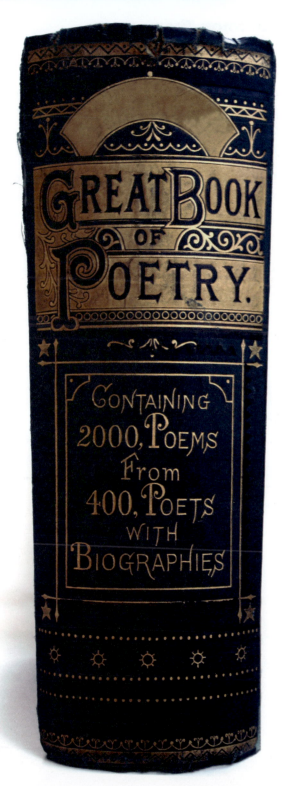

Exam Preparation

Practise comparing different poems. Pick out different pairs of poems and write down the similarities and differences you can see between them. This may be theme, layout (structure), setting or the way language is used (style).

Comparing Poems

Common Themes

The following points describe some common themes in the poems. If one of these themes came up in the exam question, you will need to think of one or two poems that cover that particular theme. The list of poems underneath each theme shows the poems that you could use.

- **Origins and Cultural Identities (where you come from)** – *Limbo, Nothing's Changed, Island Man, Search for My Tongue, Unrelated Incidents, This Room, Presents from My Aunts in Pakistan*, and *Hurricane Hits England*.
- **The difficulty of belonging to two different cultures** – *Island Man, Search for My Tongue, Presents from My Aunts in Pakistan*, and *Hurricane Hits England*.
- **Anger at discrimination and racial prejudice in society** – *Nothing's Changed, Two Scavengers in a Truck, Two Beautiful People in a Mercedes, Unrelated Incidents, Half-Caste*, and *Not My Business*.
- **Alienation (being left out and feeling alone)** – *Nothing's Changed, Search for My Tongue, Presents from My Aunts in Pakistan*, and *Hurricane Hits England*.
- **The strength of childhood memories** – *Nothing's Changed, Night of the Scorpion, Presents from My Aunts in Pakistan*, and *Hurricane Hits England*.

- **Respect for ancient traditions / cultures / language** – *Limbo, Night of the Scorpion, Unrelated Incidents, Search for My Tongue, Presents from My Aunts in Pakistan*, and *Hurricane Hits England*.
- **Survival in spite of circumstances** – *Limbo, Blessing, Night of the Scorpion, Love After Love*, and *This Room*.
- **Acceptance of who you are** – *Love After Love, This Room, Presents from My Aunts in Pakistan*, and *Hurricane Hits England*.
- **Describing places in detail** – *Blessing, Night of the Scorpion, This Room*, and *Presents from My Aunts in Pakistan*.
- **Basic lifestyles and close communities** – *Blessing* and *Night of the Scorpion*.
- **Expressing emotions through the language that is used (style)** – Many of the poems use language in a particular way to portray certain emotions.

The questions in this section of the exam usually ask you to compare how language is used to portray something within two or more of the poems. It may ask you to describe how language is used to express any of the themes above.

See pages 72 and 73 for how to answer a typical exam question on poetry from different cultures.

Exam Tips and Exam Practice

EXAM ROOM

Before the exam, make sure that you...
- know the poems well. Read each one through at least six times and make sure you know the meanings of any unfamiliar words
- learn the key points covered in this section of the guide
- are able to write confidently about content, setting, themes and style.

In the exam, make sure that you...
- read the questions carefully: take note of small words such as 'and' and 'or' (e.g. 'Compare the ways language *and* layout are used...')
- choose a question you fully understand and are confident about answering well
- underline the key words in the question to help you focus on answering it successfully
- follow the bullet points given in the question - they are there to help you
- are aware of the time: you only have 45 minutes to write your answer.

Interpreting the Question

The following words and phrases often appear in the exam questions. Make sure you understand what they mean.

'The ideas'	Refers to the poem's themes.
'An event'	Refers to something that happens in the poem(s).
'Compare...'	Write about more than one poem – do not focus on just one.
'Contrast...'	Write about noticeable differences between two or more poems.
'Your response...'	What do you think the poem is about? Comment on what you have learned about the content, setting, themes and style.
'Your reaction...'	How does the poem make you feel when you read it? Comment on the themes and style of the poem.
'The methods used...'	Write about the words and stylistic features used.
'Ways things are described...'	Write about the words and stylistic features used to describe something, someone or somewhere.
'What the poems are about'	Write about the content and themes of the poems.

Exam Practice

Answer each of the questions below in 45 minutes and ask your teacher to grade them. Remember to highlight the key words and use the 'PEE' technique (see pages 14 and 50).

1. Compare the ways in which the poets look at the difficulties in belonging to two cultures in *Presents from My Aunts in Pakistan* and one other poem. Compare...
   - how feelings about personal identity are portrayed in the poems
   - how the poets show the importance of being yourself
   - how language is used to illustrate these feelings and ideas.

2. Compare the ways in which the poets use language to comment on society in *Unrelated Incidents* and one other poem. Compare...
   - how language is used in each poem
   - how the poets use language to express their ideas
   - what you think about the issues raised in the two poems.

Developing Your Answer

In the exam you will have to write about two poems. You can write about them one at a time, but ideally you should try to write about them simultaneously (at the same time). Remember that you only have 45 minutes to write your answer.

Q. Write about the ways in which two poems describe incidents or events. Make sure you…

1. Say what incident or event is described.
2. Compare the language used to describe the incident or event.

1 Say what incident or event is described.

The writing frame below provides an example of how you might structure the beginning of your answer.

It identifies which two poems are going to be used and clearly addresses the first part of the question.

The annotation boxes contain tips on what to include a each stage.

---

1. Write about the ways in which two poems describe incidents or events. Make sure you…

    • say what incident or event is described.
    • compare the language used to describe the incident or event.

Introduction: clearly state what you are going to do.
• Refer back to the question.
• Identify the two poems you will discuss.

I am going to write about the events that are described in 'Blessing' and 'Night of the Scorpion', and look at the ways in which language is used to describe the events in these poems…

'Blessing' describes what happens in a small Indian village when a water pipe bursts and water is released into the streets. Water is such a rare commodity that it causes great excitement, especially amongst the children…

Give a brief summary of what each poem is about.

In 'Night of the Scorpion' the poet describes what happens on the night that his mother is bitten by a scorpion…

Make it clear why you have chosen those particular poems in response to the question.

I have chosen these poems because they describe two very different events and have a completely different tone, which will make an interesting comparison…

1

2 **Compare the language used to describe the incident or event.**

To answer the second part of the question it is necessary to look closely at the language used in both poems and make comparisons between the two.

Below are some examples of how you might do this.

Exam Practice

Practise using the PEE (point, evidence, explanation) technique. You will need to use it in the exam! Look at *Blessing* and *Night of the Scorpion* in your anthology and for each point made below, choose a quote (evidence) to illustrate that point and write an explanation of how it does so.

Use the PEE technique to make a point. These examples give a few of the points you could make about the use of language in these poems.

You *must* use a quote from the poem to provide evidence for every point you make and explain how the quote supports the point you are making.

In Blessing, the poet appeals to our senses [add evidence and explanation]...

Onomatopoeia is used [add evidence and explanation]...

Adjectives are used effectively in 'Night of the Scorpion' to describe the scene vividly [add evidence and explanation]...

As the night progresses more people come to help and repetition is used to emphasise the hustle and bustle of the scene [add evidence and explanation]...

The rain in 'Night of the Scorpion' contrasts with the opening of 'Blessing' [add evidence and explanation]...

In both poems, the authors create a sense of community [add evidence and explanation]...

Religious imagery runs throughout the poem 'Blessing' [add evidence and explanation]. Religious diction is also used in 'Night of the Scorpion' [add evidence and explanation]...

Both poems end with a reference to religion [add evidence and explanation]...

Both poems describe an event but they end with a wider comment [add evidence and explanation]...

The two poems, 'Blessing' and 'Night of the Scorpion', describe very different events. They both use detailed description and different features of language such as adjectives and religious imagery to enable the reader to picture the scene vividly. However, the overall tone of the two poems is very different...

2

Use the correct language terms when you make your points.

Draw comparisons between the poems.

Look at the differences as well as the similarities.

Conclusion: summarise the key points you have made in the main paragraphs (e.g. the language methods used) and relate them to both of the poems.

Writing to Inform, Explain or Describe

The Exam Question

Section B of Paper 2 will test you on your writing skills. It will contain three or four questions, of which you have to answer **one**. It is recommended that you spend 45 minutes on this question: five minutes for planning, 35 for the actual writing and five for checking. The questions cover three different types of writing:

- writing to inform
- writing to explain
- writing to describe.

Although these three types of writing are closely related, there are differences between them, which are discussed on the next page. Usually, there is one question for each of the three purposes. There may also be a fourth question combining two of the three types of writing (e.g. inform and explain).

This section of the revision guide will look at writing to inform and writing to explain together, as they have many similarities (see pages 76-85). Writing to describe is quite different and will be covered separately (see pages 86-93).

What is the examiner looking for?

The examiner wants to know how well you can write in English. Therefore, many of the marking criteria are the same as for Section B of Paper 1 (writing to argue, persuade or advise - see page 28), but the differences are in the purpose of the writing. You must be able to do the following:

- Keep the reader interested in what you say and how you say it by communicating effectively in writing and using a variety of language techniques.
- Write in clear paragraphs, ordered so that the whole piece makes sense and can be easily followed.
- Use a range of punctuation correctly, including full stops, commas, questions marks, apostrophes, inverted commas (speech marks) and exclamation marks (but use these sparingly!).
- Spell words correctly, including complex words that follow patterns and some more unusual words.
- Use vocabulary 'for effect'; do not always choose the most simple and obvious words, but think carefully about the meaning you want to put across.
- Write well in different forms.
- Always write in Standard English.
- Make the purpose of your writing clear.
- Make it clear which audience you are writing for.
- Write neatly and organise your work so that the examiner can read your writing and understand which question your answer relates to.

Writing to Inform

Wadefield High School

Dear Parent/Guardian,

I am writing to inform you about some important events in the coming term. Year 11 pupils will commence study leave on 20 May. Half term will be from Monday 29 May until Friday 2 June. Monday 5 June will be an INSET day for the staff.

Wadefield High School, 115 Broad Street, Upperthong, Wadefield WD1 1TT
t: 01924 683377   f: 01924 683378   e: wadefieldhighschool@co.uk

Writing to Explain

METALS

Metals are good conductors. Conduction occurs in metals because as the metal becomes hotter its vibrating ions gain more kinetic energy.

Science   27

Writing to Describe

Lake Garda

Lake Garda is Italy's largest lake, a beautiful expanse of blue, originally created by glaciation. The glorious surrounding scenery varies from dramatic snow-capped mountains to tranquil sandy shores and soft vine-covered hills.

Writing to Inform

Informing involves telling people the facts about a subject. Afterwards they should know more about that subject than they did before. You must…

- present the readers with a clear set of facts
- communicate the facts in a way that is easy for the readers to understand
- write from a non-biased point of view.

The letter opposite, from a head teacher to parents, is an example of writing to inform. It informs the reader what will happen; the writer does not have to argue a case or persuade the reader but may go on to explain certain things in more detail.

Writing to Explain

Explaining involves going further than simply giving information. An explanation tells people more about the subject of the writing, saying how something works or why something is as it is. You must…

- present the readers with a set of facts
- provide clear, detailed explanations of the facts
- write from a non-biased point of view.

The extract opposite, from a science book, explains why and how conduction occurs in metals (it firstly informs the reader that conduction can occur in metals).

Writing to Describe

Describing involves saying what something is like. You still inform your readers about it, but descriptive writing tends to be more personal. You must…

- provide the readers with facts
- use descriptive language techniques (adjectives etc.)
- help the readers to build up a picture in their minds.

The extract opposite, from a travel book, is an example of writing to describe. It describes the lake. It lets you imagine what it looks like by giving you information and explaining why it looks like it does. However the emphasis is on description.

You can see how closely the three types of writing are linked. Whichever question you answer in the exam, your writing will include elements of informing, explaining and describing. The difference is one of emphasis. You must consider the purpose of your writing and how this affects the way you write.

Purpose, Audience, Form and Language

This section of the book will focus on writing to inform and writing to explain.

Remember, the first things you need to know when starting to write are…

- **What is the purpose of the writing?**
  What are you trying to achieve through the writing?
- **Who is your audience?**
  Who are you writing for? Do you know the person? How old is he / she?

Purpose

Here are some examples of the type of questions you could get asked in this section of the exam:

Q. Write a letter to your MP **informing** him / her about what it is like to be a young person living in your area. Remember to…
- write a letter
- use language suitable for an MP
- inform the MP.

Q. People often find it difficult to understand why others spend their leisure time in the way they do. Write **informatively** about your favourite leisure pursuit.

Q. If you could meet anyone who had ever lived, who would it be? **Explain** the reasons for your choice.

The type of writing you are asked to do in each of the exam questions appears in bold and is therefore very clear.

In the first two questions you are asked to write about experiences. To write in an interesting way about these experiences you might need to explain why or how things happen, and give your own feelings and opinions, but the emphasis is on informing. You could even be asked to inform people about something personal, such as a forthcoming wedding but you still need to focus on informing.

The third question asks about your feelings and opinions. You still need to inform - you cannot expect the reader to know all about the person you would like to meet - but the focus is on explaining. The purpose of your writing is to help readers to understand why you want to meet a certain person. You could get a question which asks you to explain something impersonal, like how to use the Internet, but you still need to focus on explaining.

Exam Preparation

Read this question, which asks for both information and explanation, and say how it differs from the three questions opposite:

Q. Choose something you feel strongly about. Write **informatively** about it and **explain** why you feel as you do. Remember to:
- choose something you feel strongly about
- choose language to inform
- explain why you feel as you do.

Helpful Hint

If the purpose of the writing is to inform, focus on who, what, when and where.

If the purpose of the writing is to explain, focus on how and why.

join the family

We were wondering if you'd like to join the innocent family. Don't worry – it's not some weird cult. It's just our way of staying in touch with the people who drink our drinks i.e. you. Every week we'll email you our news and give you the chance to win lots of drinks. We'll also invite you to nice events like Fruitstock (our free festival) and maybe even send you the odd present if you're lucky.

If you fancy joining, visit www.innocentdrinks.co.uk/family

Audience

When you consider how to write for your audience, ask yourself…

- do I know the people I am writing to / for?
- how old are they?
- what do I have in common with them?
- what response am I trying to get from them?

Form

You may be asked to write in a specific form. This could be a letter, a leaflet, an article etc. (See pages 80-83.)

Language

The language you write in must be appropriate for the audience; you need to use the correct register. Register is the tone of voice and level of formality you use when speaking and writing. The answers to the questions above (about audience) should help you decide on the register of your writing: is it formal and businesslike or informal and chatty?

Informal Language and Register

When writing for people your age your register will be informal. You might not know them personally, but you have a lot in common with them and this will influence your language. You might…

- address them directly, using the second person ('you'), and the first person ('I' or 'we') to show that you are one of them
- use abbreviations and contractions such as 'you've' or 'mustn't'

- use the kind of vocabulary you use when talking to your friends, but don't overdo it and do not use 'text language' unless asked to do so
- use alliteration, similes or rhyme to keep it lively.

Formal Language and Register

An older audience, like your teachers, probably wouldn't appreciate an informal tone and might not take you seriously. For a formal tone, you should…

- use the second person, but not as often or in such a familiar way, e.g. use 'you might be interested to know…', rather than 'did you know that…?'
- use full words, not abbreviations or contractions, e.g. use 'did not' rather than 'didn't'
- avoid slang
- use a variety of punctuation, but avoid exclamation marks
- use more complex sentences and a variety of connectives, such as 'however' (see page 94)
- use the passive voice (e.g. 'very few bins are provided' rather than 'there aren't enough bins') to create a less personal tone
- be polite, using phrases such as 'I would be grateful if…'.

Helpful Hint

Purpose, audience, form and language are all important factors to consider when writing. Bear in mind that purpose and form, as well as audience, will also affect the type of language you use. Use the FLAP mnemonic to help you: **F**orm **L**anguage **A**udience **P**urpose. (See page 31.)

Planning Your Answer

You should spend about five minutes in the exam planning your answer. There are many ways to create a plan, including using lists and writing frames (see pages 32-33). A plan helps you decide what to include in your answer and will ensure that the points you cover are in a logical order.

When writing to inform or explain, a good way to decide what to include in your answer is to try answering six basic questions about your subject:

1 What?
2 Who?
3 Where?
4 When?
5 How?
6 Why?

These questions cover all the points that the reader will want to know. They also provide you with a good tool for planning your answer. You could jot down the questions and note some brief answers. For example, you might produce Plan 1 (opposite) in response to this question:

Q: What is your hobby? **Explain** why you enjoy this hobby.

This plan shows that there is plenty of material on which to base a good answer. The next step is to organise the answer. You could use the questions as a guide and write about each in turn, but this is not the best way to interest your reader. It is usually better to mix it up a bit, starting with a good opening paragraph that makes the reader want to know more.

Plan 2 (opposite) is a paragraph plan for the same piece of writing. This plan covers all the questions, giving both information and explanation, and shows that the writer has plenty to say on the subject.

Plan 1

- What? Dancing - Ballroom and Latin
- Who? Me, my sister, my dance teacher, other students - lots of people!
- Where? Opal Dance School - competitions all over Britain
- When? Every Saturday, Wednesday. Since I was eight
- How? Basics of dances, rehearsal, steps, music, costumes
- Why? Enjoyment, exercise, competitions

Plan 2

1. Opening - the excitement of my big competition
2. How and why I first got involved - Opal
3. The popularity of dance and all the different types there are.
4. Latin dancing and Ballroom dancing - the differences
5. My favourite dance - what it involves and why I like it
6. Costumes and music
7. Competitions
8. The big competition and how it turned out

What should you write about?

'Write about what you know.' This is the advice that is often given to writers. It is especially useful when deciding on the subject matter of your exam answer.

Choice

Some questions do not offer a lot of choice. For example, if you are asked to write an article giving information about GCSE options at your school, you can only write about the options that exist. But if you are asked to give a report on an event, there may be several different events you could choose from - national events, school events, family events etc.

Interest and Involvement

If you are asked to write about something like an event, choose a real event that you were involved with and that you found interesting, exciting or funny. There is no point writing about an event you weren't involved with, as you will not be able to say much about it. Equally, if you were involved in an event that you found very boring, your writing is unlikely to interest your readers.

Personal Subjects

If you are asked about more personal subjects, for example your hobbies, try to choose something that you really enjoy doing. That way, you will have the knowledge to explain your subject in a detailed and interesting way, and your enthusiasm will come through in your writing. Often when pupils say that they find writing difficult or boring, it is because they are writing about subjects that don't interest them. So if you spot a question that gives you the chance to write about something that you really care about, do it!

Helpful Hint

Always remember to write in paragraphs; your ideas and explanations will be clearer and will make more sense. The examiner wants to see that you can structure your ideas.

Exam Preparation

Create a plan, using the six basic questions, for a discursive essay about your favourite hobby. (Have you got enough material for a two-page essay?)

Structure and Form: Articles

This section of the exam often has a question which asks you to write an article. This may be an article for a newspaper, a magazine or a website. (See pages 37-39 for more on writing articles.)

If you look at articles for these three media, you will see that the differences between them are to do with audience as well as purpose. All three media run articles to inform, explain or describe things to their readers. The style and tone of these articles depend on the subject and the intended audience as well as on their purpose.

Presentation

As with any piece of writing, you should set out your work in paragraphs (see pages 35 and 36). You should also use the following features of newspaper and magazine articles:

A headline: this is the title of the article. It may be serious or funny and often uses language features like puns, alliteration or rhyme. For example,

> Winter Wonderland

This headline uses alliteration to grab the reader's attention, but it does not say what the article is actually about.

A strapline: this comes just above or below the headline and introduces the story, explaining the headline.
For example,

> Santa's grotto and delicious festive fare add a flavour of Christmas as part of the annual celebrations.

This explains what the article will be about (Christmas celebrations), and attracts readers by using alliteration ('festive fare'), and a metaphor ('a flavour of Christmas') to give a sense of excitement and enjoyment.

Sub-headings: these are used to organise and break up the text, making it easy to follow and allowing the reader to skip to the bits that interest him / her most.

Each sub-heading may introduce two or three paragraphs. Sub-headings can also help your planning. Note down the most important things you want to write about, and then put them in order. For example, planning for a football report might look something like this:

Grudge match against Sutton	1	Hartson's header	3
Half time honours even	4	Penalty joy	7
Sutton scores first	2	Smithy scores	5
Sutton captain sent off	6	Freshfields in final	8

These rough notes could make effective sub-headings, helping to create a lively and engaging article. The numbers give the order of the sub-headings.

Exam Practice

Answer the following question in 45 minutes.

Q. Write an article for the school newsletter in which you **inform** parents about a forthcoming sports event at your school. Remember to:
- write an article
- use language suitable for parents
- inform the parents.

Helpful Hint

Presentation is not important, as long as the examiner can read your writing. You will not get extra marks for trying to make your work look like a real newspaper article with columns and pictures; you may even lose marks because it wastes time and distracts the examiner from the content of your writing.

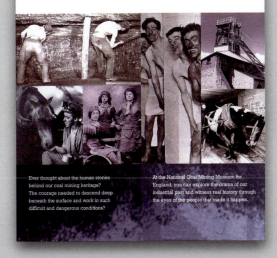

It is not often that a question comes up in this section of the exam which asks you to write a leaflet or information sheet - but it might happen. (See page 40 for more on leaflets.) If you choose to answer such a question, don't waste time trying to make your answer paper look like a real leaflet, but do think about using headlines, straplines and sub-headings (see pages 80 and 37-39).

If you are asked to write a leaflet in this section of the exam its purpose will probably be to inform (though it might also include explaining or describing something).

Problems with Writing Leaflets

The biggest problem that students find with informative writing for leaflets is the fact that real leaflets tend to be written in simple language and often use presentational devices such as bullet points. It can be hard, therefore, to use the range of language that achieves good marks. Also, if you are simply telling people facts, there is not much room for developing a distinctive style in your writing.

Make sure you give the information clearly, but also try to explain things in greater detail. Try to use language that will make your piece interesting and entertaining, perhaps by including alliteration, rhyme, puns, metaphors or similes.

Helpful Hint

Whatever form your writing takes, make sure you always use paragraphs (see pages 35 and 36). Paragraphs break up your writing into organised chunks which makes your ideas easier to follow. The examiners expect you to use paragraphs in your writing.

Exam Preparation

Next time you are out, pick up some free leaflets (you could also look in the post for junk mail) and look at what the leaflets are informing you about. Do they also contain explanation and/or description? See if you can find examples of alliteration, rhyme, puns, metaphors or similes in the leaflets.

Structure and Form: Letters

Writing in the form of a letter might come up in this section of the exam.

Whatever form you are asked to write in, you must consider your audience and the appropriate tone. If you are writing a letter, the identity of your audience will influence how you set it out and how you begin and end.

Informal Letters

If you wanted to write to a friend, a relative or someone you know very well you would write an informal letter. You would use the person's first name and end with an informal 'signing off'. Look at example 1 (opposite).

Formal Letters

If you wanted to write to a teacher, an employer, a newspaper editor, or someone you don't know well, you would write a formal letter. You should address the recipient formally, and sign off your letter formally ('yours faithfully' or 'yours sincerely'). A person whose name you do not know is addressed as 'sir or madam'. Look at example 2 (opposite).

Helpful Hint

When writing a formal letter, if you write 'Dear Sir / Madam', sign off with 'Yours faithfully'. If you write the recipient's name (e.g. Dear Mrs Ellman'), sign off with 'Yours sincerely'.

Exam Preparation

Here is part of a formal letter to the school governors informing them about the school's litter problem. Rewrite this text to create a new letter to be sent to your fellow students:

> We students have become very concerned lately about the amount of litter to be found around the school. Almost every day, students arrive in their classrooms to find the floors are covered in sweet wrappers, empty crisp packets and discarded drink cans. The corridors are even worse. Very few bins are provided and those are overflowing with litter…

Example 1

Dear Kayleigh

Thanks for my brilliant birthday present. I love it! It's my favourite perfume so I'm really pleased!

Sorry you couldn't make it to my birthday party – it would have been fab to see you. But thanks so much for sending me a card and the present.

I'll ring you in the next few weeks and we'll arrange to meet up.

See you soon,

Love, Jane

xxx

Example 2

6 Moorland Road
Greenham
Derbyshire

Mr J Johnson
Manager
Greenham Bank
134 High Street
Greenham

12th May

Dear Mr Johnson

I am writing to inform you of my change of address. As of the 24th of June, my address will be as follows:

69 Oaktree Close
Leafdale
Greenham
Derbyshire
DB5 24F

Please amend my details to take account of this change of address. My telephone number will remain the same. If you need any further details, don't hesitate to contact me.

Yours sincerely

Jane Reid

Jane Reid

Structure and Form: Discursive Essays

Articles, letters and leaflets are specific forms in which you may be asked to write. However, in recent years more than half the questions in the writing to inform, explain or describe section have asked for 'discursive writing' or a traditional essay. This means that you are not told to write in a specific form or for a specific audience.

Here are two examples of this type of question which may come up in this section of the exam:

Q. **Explain** how you feel at the moment and why you feel this way.

Q. Think about something you made that you were proud of. **Explain** how you made it and what your feelings were about it.

These two questions have two things in common; they both ask you to explain something, and they both ask you to write about personal matters.

If you decide to answer this type of question in the exam, set out your work in paragraphs as you would for any piece of writing. The structure and content of your work will be very similar to any other 'inform' or 'explain' answer. For example, it will still help you to make a plan of your answer so that the points you make are in a logical order.

The main difference between discursive essay writing and writing in other forms is that you are less likely to use the second person ('you') in discursive essays. You might use it in the introduction to grab the reader's attention, or as part of a rhetorical question. However it should be used sparingly; you do not know who your audience is so it is difficult to address them directly.

Helpful Hint

When you read the exam questions, do not ignore small words such as 'and' and 'or'. These words can make all the difference in how you interpret the question. For example, the second question (opposite) asks you to write about how you made something *and* your feelings about it - it does not ask for one or the other.

Exam Practice

Answer the following question in 45 minutes.

Q. Think of a time when you were very frightened and **explain** why you felt that way.

Personal and Impersonal Writing

■ Whatever form of writing the question asks for (article, letter, essay etc.), a good answer will include elements of both personal and impersonal writing.

■ Personal Writing

Personal writing is when you are writing about yourself. The most personal type of writing is in a diary, where you put down your most private thoughts. Autobiographies and letters to friends are other examples of personal writing.

■ Anecdotes

You may use anecdotes in your writing to make it more personal. Anecdotes are very brief personal stories, often amusing, and used to illustrate a point. They are very useful for introducing your subject. Look at this introduction to an essay on dancing in response to the question: What is your hobby? **Explain** why you enjoy this hobby.

> It was the biggest night of my life so far. I could feel my heart pounding with excitement. I checked my make-up in the dressing room mirror: fine. I checked my hair: fine. Then I looked down at my shoes: disaster!
>
> I was performing with the other students from Opal, my local dance school…

This opening uses personal writing (the anecdote). to 'hook' the reader.

Always remember however, what the question is asking you to do – explain and inform. It demands that you tell the readers things they did not know, not just about you, but about your hobby. To do this you also need to include an impersonal element.

In the essay plan on page 78 the tone switches from personal to impersonal in the third paragraph, which opens up the essay so that it is no longer just about the writer but about dancing in general. Here you could make use of facts you have learned; you could discuss the history and origins of dancing, give statistics, perhaps about the number of dance schools in the country or the number of people who go to classes, and even give information about physiology learned in PE lessons.

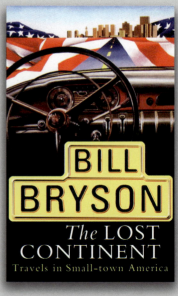

Impersonal Writing

Impersonal writing is when you are not writing about yourself. You may be writing about an event, a place, a country, a person (other than yourself or your friends and family), an activity etc. that has nothing to do with you. A newspaper article about a break-in at an office is an example of impersonal writing.

Impersonal Writing Tips

- When the tone is impersonal there will be less use of the first person and more use of the third person (e.g. 'people all over the country enjoy dance lessons' rather than 'I enjoy dance lessons').
- There may be impersonal constructions such as the passive voice (e.g. 'the tango was first introduced to Europe from Argentina').
- Even though the writing is impersonal, your style can still be lively and entertaining - and you can still include a personal viewpoint - just as long as you are clear that you are giving information and explanations. The reader should come away knowing more about the subject than he / she did before.
- Show that you have a lot of information, drawn from various sources, and sound as if you know what you are talking about.

Exam Preparation

What are you an expert on? What do you know a lot about? Write an opening paragraph and a second paragraph for a discursive essay.

Write the opening paragraph in a personal tone that will invite the reader into your world. (You could try to use an anecdote.) Write the second paragraph in an impersonal tone to give information or an explanation.

Purpose, Audience and Form

This section of the book will focus on writing to describe.

Purpose

The main difference between writing to inform or explain and writing to describe is that describe questions give you the opportunity to be more creative and really use your imagination. You can use a wide vocabulary and a variety of sentence structures for effect. You can show your own style and create something really original.

You must not write a story. There may be an element of narrative writing in your work but the focus is on description, not plot. You could be asked to describe a place, a person or an experience. Here are some examples of the type of questions you might get:

Q. **Describe** your ideal holiday.

Q. **Describe** a place where you enjoy spending your time.

Q. Think of a recent trip you have taken and **describe** how you got to your destination.

Q. **Describe** a park in the summer and describe it in the winter. Remember to...
- describe the park in the summer
- describe the park in the winter
- use language suitable for describing.

All four of these questions can be answered in different ways.
- An 'ideal holiday' could be a holiday you have been on, one you have heard about, or the kind of holiday you would like to have in the future and can only dream about now.
- A 'place where you enjoy spending your time', could be a real place like a leisure centre or your bedroom, or it could be a fantasy world full of magical and exotic sights and sounds.
- The question about journeys is a bit different as it asks you to write about 'a recent trip you have taken', suggesting it must be a real experience. But if you feel that you have never been on a trip that was interesting enough to write about, you can pretend that you are someone else, or make one up, and let your imagination run wild.
- The fourth question asks for two descriptions of the same place. Other questions could ask you to describe somewhere at night and in the morning, or in the past and the future. You could write two separate descriptions, one after the other, or you could write alternate paragraphs on each scene, comparing as you go.

Helpful Hint

Do not answer a writing to describe question by writing a story; you will not do well.

Exam Preparation

Take each of the four questions on this page and 'brainstorm' at least three different places/experiences that you could describe for each answer.

Example 1

> 26 Hill View
> Norwich
> Norfolk
>
> Dear Claire
>   That gloomy old house on the corner has changed beyond recognition: where there was dark green ivy, there are now roses blushing pink in the sun: instead of an overgrown jungle of a front garden, there is a Mediterranean style patio with neat potted shrubs and gleaming concrete.

Example 2

> 26 Hill View
> Norwich
> Norfolk
>
> Dear Tom
>   The house next to ours is the corner house. It is larger than all the others in the street and used to belong to an old lady. It seemed to reflect her personality and age, with trailing ivy surrounding the front door and a jungle of weeds for a front garden. But now it has new owners and has changed beyond recognition.

Audience

Questions on writing to describe do not usually specify an audience but you might get a question like this:

Q. Write a letter to a pen friend who lives abroad, **describing** the area in which you live.

Just as with inform and explain questions, if the describe question specifies an audience, you should ask yourself questions about the intended audience (see page 77).

Imagine you are asked to write a description of your neighbourhood for an old friend who has moved away. She knows the area so you do not have to describe everything in great detail. She would probably only be interested in changes to the neighbourhood.

Look at example 1 (opposite). The references to what the house used to look like show that the reader must have some prior knowledge of it.

If on the other hand, you are writing for an American pen friend who has never visited you, you might explain a bit more, as in example 2 (opposite).

So in example 1 the writer assumes that the reader knows 'the gloomy old house'. He / she does not need to explain where it is or who it belongs to. In example 2 the writer provides background information to give the reader a more complete picture.

Form

You may be asked to write a description in a particular form, e.g. an article for a magazine or newspaper or a letter, like the example on this page (see pages 80-83 for how to write in different forms). Usually, however, a describe question will not specify a particular form.

Exam Preparation

Try writing a paragraph about the house on the corner for an alien from another planet. The alien knows nothing about life on earth so you will have to try to see it as the alien would!

Planning Your Answer

Sometimes people have difficulty knowing how to approach a piece of descriptive writing. Too often they write a narrative (a story). The problem with this is that you end up spending your time working out a 'plot', which you will not get marks for if you have not described things in detail.

Often when pupils write descriptions of real places they waste time explaining how they got there: for example, if they are describing a place they have been to on holiday, they mention everything from getting up in the morning and boarding the plane to arriving home a week later.

You need to think about what you are being asked to describe and focus on that.

Big to Small Technique

An effective way to plan a piece of descriptive writing is to go from 'big to small'. Imagine you are a camera gradually zooming in on an object. Start by describing something big, for example, a building, in general terms. As you get closer and more involved, your description becomes more detailed, until you focus on something small but significant. Opposite is a 'big to small' plan of an answer based on the question about a place where you enjoy spending your time.

A piece of writing based on this plan would keep readers interested by bringing them gradually into the world being described. It is as if the reader is being brought to the house and shown round it.

See pages 32 and 78-79 for other ways to plan your answer.

My Grandparents' House

Paragraph 1:	Its location: far away from the city ➝ by the sea
Paragraph 2:	The approach to the house: the lane ➝ the front garden ➝ looking at the house
Paragraph 3:	The house's layout: number of rooms ➝ the style of décor of the rooms
Paragraph 4:	The kitchen ➝ old-fashioned appliances; the living room ➝ small, comfortable ➝ fireplace
Paragraph 5:	The people in the house: grandparents welcoming me ➝ memories
Paragraph 6:	Me in my bedroom: my shelves ➝ my books
Paragraph 7:	How I would feel when I wake up in the morning ➝ what I see, hear, smell etc.

Using the Senses

Another good way of planning your descriptive piece is to use the five senses. A good descriptive piece uses all five senses: sight, sound, smell, touch and taste.

Left is an example of a plan using the senses, based on the question: 'Think of a recent trip you have taken and describe how you got to your destination'.

The writer has chosen to describe a train journey through a foreign country on the way to visit a relative.

The next step is to put his / her thoughts in order. This is easy, as a journey has a beginning, middle and an end. The writer also has to decide when to begin and end the writing. It could start when he / she left home, but that would mean more informing and less describing, and the journey does not become interesting until he / she gets to the station.

The next step is to do a paragraph plan to decide what goes in each paragraph. The words and phrases in the plan opposite have been numbered to fit into the paragraph plan below.

1. The city: railway station → reason for journey
2. The train: settling in on the train → people
   → foreign languages
3. Through the window: city, industry, suburbs, mountains
4. The lady opposite: her story → sharing
   lunch → food
5. Arrival: being met at the village station.

Exam Preparation

1 Write a 'big to small' plan for a completely different interpretation of the 'place where you enjoy spending your time' question. You could use these ideas for the opening paragraph:
- a busy shop in the town centre
- a log cabin in the Alps.

2 Choose two questions from page 86. For each of the questions try doing a plan based on the senses, including 'my feelings' as a 'sixth' sense.

Decide how you would organise your answer and create a paragraph plan.

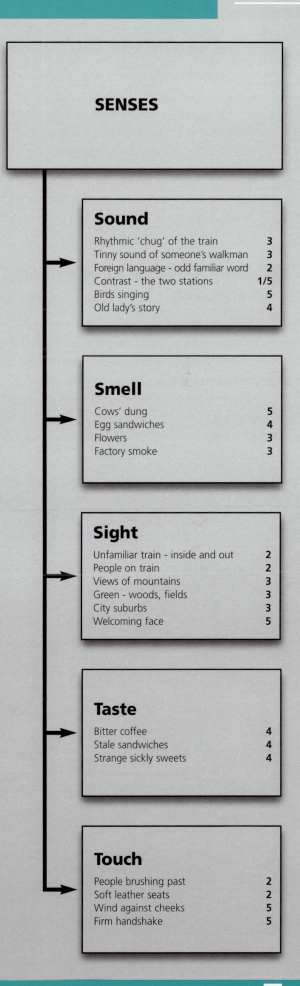

SENSES

Sound

Rhythmic 'chug' of the train	3
Tinny sound of someone's walkman	3
Foreign language - odd familiar word	2
Contrast - the two stations	1/5
Birds singing	5
Old lady's story	4

Smell

Cows' dung	5
Egg sandwiches	4
Flowers	3
Factory smoke	3

Sight

Unfamiliar train - inside and out	2
People on train	2
Views of mountains	3
Green - woods, fields	3
City suburbs	3
Welcoming face	5

Taste

Bitter coffee	4
Stale sandwiches	4
Strange sickly sweets	4

Touch

People brushing past	2
Soft leather seats	2
Wind against cheeks	5
Firm handshake	5

Choosing Your Subject

What should you write about?

Where possible, try to write about something you enjoy. As with answers to inform and explain questions, this can mean writing about what you know, but in the case of descriptive writing, you might prefer to use your imagination.

Most questions for writing to describe leave you plenty of scope to decide on your own subject. You could use your memories, or you could create a new and imaginative world of your own.

Using Personal or Impersonal Language

Sometimes the question will have the word 'you' in it, perhaps asking you to describe your experience, or to describe a place or person that means a lot to you. In such cases, you should use the first person ('I', 'we') in your writing. Other questions will simply ask you to describe something or somebody. These can be answered in a personal or impersonal way. Compare the following two descriptions.

> Lake Garda is Italy's largest lake, a beautiful expanse of blue originally created by glaciation. The glorious surrounding scenery varies from dramatic snow-capped mountains to tranquil sandy shores and soft vine-covered hills. This stunning setting has led to Lake Garda becoming one of Italy's most popular tourist destinations, an ideal spot for sunbathing and water sports.

> The sunset was the most beautiful I had seen; an array of colour across the sky that reflected into the sea and glistened on the peaceful waves. I watched as the blue sky turned to a pale purple, then pink and orange, like an endless rainbow. I don't know how long I was sitting there. I knew the others would be looking for me, but the view was so magnificent I was transfixed.

While both pieces describe beautiful places, they are very different in tone.

The first is written in the third person ('he', 'she', 'it', 'they') which makes it sound as if facts are being given rather than opinions.

The second is written in the first person and the reader is very aware of the character and what the view means to him / her. Both would be good answers to a question asking for a description of a favourite place, or a good holiday destination.

Writing about People

You may be asked to describe a person. It could be someone who has inspired you, someone you know well or perhaps a stranger who interests you. This sort of writing can be very personal, and your relationship with that person will form a big part of your answer.

- Be careful not to fall back on clichés, especially when writing about someone you love.
- Look for what is different or unusual in the person you are describing. For example, people who write about their grandparents usually say that they are lovely, kind people. This may be true, but it is not very interesting.
- Think about why you like the person, and think about anything that might amuse or intrigue the reader.

Here is a brief description of a person:

> Jack had lived in the first floor flat above the launderette for 15 years with only his dog, a scruffy terrier named Barney, for company. But he loved that dog and treated it with the same loyalty and affection that the dog showed him. Jack was an aged-looking man with dark, sun-baked skin, deep-set lines on his forehead, and small, crooked teeth that showed when he smiled. He was a quiet man, but he always smiled.

This description sketches a vivid picture of Jack in just a few lines, giving the reader information about three important aspects of him:

1. **Physical description:** 'an aged-looking man with dark, sun-baked skin...small crooked teeth...'
2. **Personality:** 'he loved that dog...affection', 'He was a quiet man...always smiled.'
3. **Background:** 'had lived in the first floor flat... for 15 years...'

You might start by giving a physical description.
- What does he / she look like - (hair, eyes, face, size)?
- What does he / she like to wear?
- How does he / she move?
- What does he / she sound like?
- Does he / she have a distinctive smell?

Then you could move on to aspects of personality and background.
- What sort of temperament does he / she have?
- What are his / her beliefs?
- Does he / she have any special interests?
- Where does he / she come from?
- What is his / her family like?

Finally, you could write about your relationship with the person and how you feel about him / her.

Exam Preparation

Try planning an answer to this question.
- **Q. Describe** a person whom you have never met, but admire. Explain why you admire him or her.

Descriptive Language Techniques

A writing to describe question gives you the chance to show that you have a wide vocabulary and that you can use it in a creative way. The success of a descriptive piece depends on your use of language.

The following are all language techniques which should be used in order to create a good descriptive piece of writing.

Adjectives

Adjectives describe nouns, telling us more about them. You will not get much credit for using very simple adjective and noun combinations, like 'a **big** house', 'an **old** lady' or 'the **loud** noise'. Look for alternatives: the house might be 'gigantic', 'imposing' or even 'gargantuan', the lady could be 'ancient', 'elderly' or 'venerable', and the noise might be 'deafening', 'piercing' or 'shrill'. Choose the adjective that is most appropriate for the noun you have in mind.

You could try using two or three adjectives before a noun, for example 'a **neglected**, **crumbling** mansion'. Use this sparingly, however, for variety.

Nouns

You can create description simply by using a good noun. For example, is your house a mansion, a bungalow, a terrace or a townhouse? If the readers know what sort of house it is they can picture it more clearly.

Adverbs

Adverbs describe verbs, telling us how something is done, e.g. 'she edged **slowly** towards the animal', 'the birds were singing **joyfully**'.

Helpful Hints

Descriptive writing often seems more alive and involving if it is written in the present tense: write about your experience as if it is happening to you (and your reader) now.

Do not think you have to put an adjective before every noun. Sometimes it is best to keep things simple.

Imagery

Imagery is the use of language to create images for the reader. Two kinds of imagery that you will have come across are **metaphors** and **similes**. Try to use these in your writing to make your descriptions more vivid and individual. Metaphors and similes tell the reader what a thing, feeling or idea means to the writer by comparing it to something else. A simile uses a word such as 'like' or 'as' to compare (e.g. 'as fierce as a lion', 'sleeping like a log'), while a metaphor suggests that one thing is the other ('he was a little angel', 'you are my sun and moon').

Onomatopoeia

Onomatopoeia is another descriptive technique: the use of words that sound like the thing being described, e.g. 'the **crackle** of leaves underfoot', 'the **hiss** of a snake' or 'the steady **chug chug** of the train'.

Alliteration

Alliteration can also have an impact. A string of words beginning with 's', for example, can create the idea of something slippery or sinister, e.g. 'slithering, snake-like they slide into the shadows'. Words beginning with a hard 'c' or 'k' can give an impression of harshness and violence, e.g. 'he clasps the crag with crooked hands'. 'P' and 'b' sounds give an impression of quick, explosive movement, e.g. 'Pete was pipped at the post'.

Repetition

Repetition can be used to emphasise an idea and give shape and pattern to a piece of writing, perhaps by starting a series of sentences with the same word, e.g, 'Darkness enveloped the street. Darkness seemed to cover the whole world that night. It was the darkness, not the cold, that made me shiver'.

Sentence Structure

You also need to consider your sentence structure. Try to mix long and short sentences; long ones for detailed descriptions that draw the reader in and short ones for impact.

Exam Preparation

Rewrite the following description, using some of the techniques discussed on these pages to make it clearer and more vivid for the reader.

> I turned the corner into the street. I could see a lot of buildings around me. It was night but there was a moon. There were people walking up and down the street, or standing in doorways. A dog barked at me. I was frightened so I started to run.

Exam Practice

Write an answer to the following question in 45 minutes.
Q. Describe a beach in summer and describe it in winter.

Exam Tips

Useful Words and Phrases

You need to show that you can link your ideas effectively, whether within sentences, between sentences or between paragraphs. Words and phrases that link ideas or events are called connectives, or discourse markers. They help your writing to flow and make sense.

Here are a few such words and phrases that could be useful in writing to inform, explain or describe:

- **To add information or build on ideas:**
  Also, In addition, Additionally, As well as, Furthermore, Moreover, Similarly
- **To introduce a contrasting idea or point of view:**
  However, Nevertheless, Although, On the other hand, Despite, In spite of, In contrast
- **To express cause and effect:**
  Because of, As a result, Therefore, Consequently
- **To give order to your ideas:**
  Firstly, Secondly, Finally, In conclusion
- **To express passing time:**
  Afterwards, Subsequently, Later, Before this, Previously, Immediately, Straightaway, The following (day etc.), As soon as, Meanwhile

Checking Your Work

You have 45 minutes to write your answer. Of this you should spend five minutes planning your answer and five minutes checking your work. Even if you feel quite confident about spelling, punctuation and grammar, it is easy to make careless errors under pressure.

Make sure you have...

- written in clear paragraphs (if you have forgotten, go back and mark clearly where each paragraph would begin – see page 35)
- linked your paragraphs with connectives such as the ones on this page and on page 34
- correctly used a variety of punctuation including full stops, commas, question marks and apostrophes
- correctly spelt simple words and complex words which follow patterns
- crossed out mistakes neatly and written in corrections clearly.

If you make mistakes with simple words or straightforward punctuation, your work cannot be given a good grade. However, you do not have to have perfect spelling and punctuation. If you are trying to be adventurous with your choice of vocabulary and sentence structure, you are likely to make a few mistakes and this is perfectly acceptable.

Make sure you read through the Common Errors: Punctuation, Grammar and Spelling on pages 4-5.

Exam Practice

Try to write an answer to each of the questions on page 86. Only allow yourself 45 minutes per question.

Index

Index